Joe Barnard is a spiritual and mor
immensely practical and persuasive
Scripture and outstanding expositors l
to offer an acute guide to self-diagnos
which to dispense with besetting sin
This is a book for men who are fed up with therapeutic ...
to walk the walk.

DAVID LYLE JEFFREY
Distinguished Senior Fellow, Baylor Institute for Studies in Religion
Emeritus Distinguished Professor of Literature and the Humanities,
Baylor University, Waco, Texas

Joe Barnard is sounding an alarm bell that men must hear. Men are in a daily battle for our hearts, minds, families and futures. Joe is helping us see that when we walk out into this culture every day, we are walking onto a battlefield. If we're unprepared, we're easy prey. I'm personally grateful for his important reminder! Armed with the gospel of Christ, we can be victorious! If you're a man who is ready to fight, this book is for you.

KENT EVANS
Author of *The Manhood Journey* and Executive Director of Manhood Journey

If you have been looking for a short book to help you understand your battle with sin, *Surviving the Trenches* is it. Joe Barnard compiles years of thinking on the topic of sin from some of the most notable Christian thinkers of all time and presents it in a simple way that will help even a new believer understand the war we wage with sin. He maintains that only God saves humanity from the clutches of sin yet perfectly explains how we play a role in waging war with the sin that never stops raging against us. I would highly recommend this book for anyone in a present battle with sin – and that's pretty much everyone.

VINCE MILLER
Author, speaker, founder of Resolute

Killing sin is a critical aspect of true discipleship that Christian men neglect at our peril. Here is wise and practical encouragement which, prayerfully and courageously applied, can change our lives for ever. An urgent call to arms!

JONATHAN LAMB
Author, teacher and minister-at-large for Keswick Ministries

Joe Barnard has shown the spotlight on one of the most neglected areas in modern Evangelicalism: The purposeful, deliberate mortification of sin in the believer's life. With tactical clarity Barnard describes the Enemy's devices and presents practical strategies for waging war with indwelling sin. *Surviving the Trenches* is a call to spiritual arms that should be read by every Christian.

REAGAN ROSE
Founder of Redeeming Productivity

Tragically, mortification is a word that has all but disappeared from our theological vocabulary. Unmortified sins devastate not only individual lives, but wreak havoc on families and churches. *Surviving in the Trenches: Killing Sin Before Sin Kills You,* appeals to the consciences of Christian men, offering them a sound biblical theology of sin as well as practical strategies for fighting it. The author targets four specific sins: pride, lust, vanity, and sloth. He exposes their deadliness, but also proclaims the hope every Christian man has in his all sufficient Savior.

CHARLES M. WINGARD
Professor of Pastoral Theology and Dean of Students,
Reformed Theological Seminary, Jackson, Mississippi

Joe Barnard provides a needed sense of urgency for the most important battle of a man's life – the battle against sin. Much more than a how-to guide for dealing with sin, *Surviving the Trenches* will transform your mindset about sin from mere life-management and problem-solving to what sin really is – a life-or-death battlefield.

KEN BOA
President of Reflections Ministry
and author of *Conformed to His Image*

Joe Barnard has a passion to see communities transformed by the power of Christ. His writing style resembles that of J. C. Ryle. He is practical, clear, and deliberate. Mortifying sin is not a popular topic today, however, it is as important as ever. Without understanding and applying the principles contained in Matthew 5:27-30, the Christian will not make much progress in their pursuit of spiritual growth.

ABEL SCHAFER
Pastor, Fellowship Bible Church, Little Rock, Arkansas

Men – stop what you are doing and order this book! This book is filled with simple statements of truth that you will not forget. The author helps us see the danger of sin, the lies of our adversary, but even more importantly, the means of escape through the Gospel and a life dedicated to battling the unseen war for our souls. We men need a wakeup call to the deceitfulness of sin, the increasing dullness of the Christian soul, and the beauty of Christ and the joys of holiness. This book delivers on all counts.

Joe Smith
Executive Director of Broken Strength: A Path to Purity

Joe Barnard writes that Christian men today are alarmingly unprepared for the daily battle against the lusts and sinful desires in each man's heart. His book *Surviving the Trenches* gives you hope that the victory over sin has already been won, but it underscores the deadliness of the battle to claim that victory as a daily personal experience. *Surviving the Trenches* deals honestly with the battle – it is difficult and dangerous, and there are no shortcuts for easy victories. As the Royal Navy maxim notes, 'If you want peace, prepare for war.' Joe's book prepares men for the battle with an insight that is learned, biblical, challenging, and captivating. From 10 rules for the battle to the lies sin uses against all of us, *Surviving the Trenches* shoots straight with a clarity that is refreshing and informative. And you will understand the battle you are in and how to persevere to claim the victory Christ has won. You won't be able to put this book down, and you can't afford to miss its message.

Bobby Crotty
Men's Equipping Director, Watermark Community Church, Dallas, Texas

Every man needs a battle plan against temptation and sin. Joe Barnard masterfully paints a pathway of how to go to war against sin – killing it – and he does so in a grace filled manner. This book will inspire men to proactively confront the hardest, yet most important fight of your life. Get ready, it just may change your life!

Josh Jordan
College Pastor, First Baptist Church, Covington, Louisiana

Joe Barnard has written a must-read primer for all pilgrims who realize they are in a spiritual war. Read this book and learn how to go to war. Joe's writing and insight are a gift to our generation of men.

Tyrell Haag
Pastor at Pineland Baptist Church, Ontario

So many believing men don't experience the freedom from sin that is promised in the Gospel. Into that struggle, Joe Barnard speaks with a refreshingly biblical and historically-rooted perspective, helping men untangle themselves from the lies they've believed and giving them a Gospel-rooted path to see victory over the sins that linger.

Jason D. Wood
Pastor, Faith Presbyterian Church, Covington, Louisiana

There is a time for straight talking. A time to grab the nettle. A time to rip-off the sticking plaster. This book is written in a similar vain. Joe tackles the subject of men waging war against sin, the flesh and the devil, head on. It is a guttural rallying cry to wake men up to the spiritual battle they are naively dawdling through. This book is very honest. The enemy may be devious, sin may be enslaving and despair may be felt, but the power of the Spirit, the truth of the Word, and the hope of the gospel are more than adequate to bolster resistance and bring renewal to even the most seemingly defeated of saints. I heartily recommend this jugular volume to all men. It will stiffen your spine, strengthen your arm and bring courage to your heart. This book is very hopeful.

Jonathan Gemmell
Co-Director of Training at Cornhill Scotland

SURVIVING THE TRENCHES

KILLING SIN BEFORE SIN KILLS YOU

JOE BARNARD

CHRISTIAN FOCUS

Scripture quotations are from *The Holy Bible, English Standard Version*, copyright © 2001 by Crossway Bibles, a division of Good News Publishers. Used by permission. All rights reserved.

Scripture quotations marked (NKJV) are taken from the *New King James Version*. Copyright © 1982 by Thomas Nelson, Inc. Used by permission. All rights reserved.

Copyright © Joe Barnard 2022

Paperback ISBN 978-1-5271-0857-8
Ebook ISBN 978-1-5271-0883-7

10 9 8 7 6 5 4 3 2 1

Published in 2022
by
Christian Focus Publications Ltd,
Geanies House, Fearn, Ross-shire,
IV20 1TW, Scotland, Great Britain

www.christianfocus.com

Cover design by James Amour

Printed and bound by Bell & Bain, Glasgow

All rights reserved. No part of this publication may be reproduced, stored in a retrieval system, or transmitted, in any form, by any means, electronic, mechanical, photocopying, recording or otherwise without the prior permission of the publisher or a licence permitting restricted copying. In the U.K. such licences are issued by the Copyright Licensing Agency, 4 Battlebridge Lane, London, SE1 2HX www.cla.co.uk.

CONTENTS

Orientation 9

1 **The Rules of War** 21

2 **The Fight against Deception** 47

3 **How to Kill an Entrenched Passion** 75

4 **Four Sins That Are Killing Modern Men** 101

Epilogue 129

Appendix 133

DEDICATION

This book is dedicated to Rusty Olps and Richard Miltenberger who gave me a first taste of spiritual friendship while sitting in a canoe on the bayous of South Louisiana.

Orientation

◁◁◁♦♦♦▷▷▷

I shudder to think of the first wave of British soldiers at the Battle of the Somme. The plan, in theory, was simple. Heavy artillery would clear a path for the advancing infantry to follow. This artillery would do three things: cut through barbed wire in no man's land, destroy enemy machine guns, and unleash a blizzard of fire on the opposing trench, obliterating the brunt of resistance. The role of the infantry in the plan was meant to be minimal. Soldiers would climb out of one trench, navigate the cleared terrain, and hop into another trench. Little hand-to-hand combat was expected. The job of foot soldiers was place-holding: guard one line of victory until the next was secured.[1]

The plan, however, was a disaster. The first problem was that the artillery was ill-timed and ineffective, unleashing a cascade of deadly consequences. As soldiers scampered over the parapets, they discovered that the German machine guns were intact and the gunners alert. Rows of British soldiers were shot down before they could figure out what was going on. Those men who did manage to reach the barbed wire stumbled into a terrifying obstacle: *The wire was not cut.* These soldiers became target practice as they frantically tried to cut their way through a thicket of mesh. A final horror awaited the

---

1. For a realistic account of the Battle of the Somme see John Keegan, *The Face of Battle: A Study of Agincourt, Waterloo, and the Somme* (New York: Penguin, 1983), ch. 4.

trickle of men who managed to crawl all of the way to the enemy line. The bombardment had failed. The German infantry was unscathed. As British soldiers reached the rim of the enemy line, they could see that, instead of leaping down into a mass grave, they were approaching a hive of combatants. Thus, like a script for a horror movie, a presumed triumph was turned into a vicious holocaust. On July 1st, 1916, day one of the Somme, the British suffered over 57,000 casualties, including nearly 20,000 fatalities. Men who had thought that they would be writing letters of heroic exploits to loved ones were instead lying crippled in make-shift hospitals or, even worse, stacked among the dead.

Little pleasure is derived from reading about the Battle of the Somme. It is painful to picture a young soldier, perhaps a teenager, leaping out of a trench, thinking that he is stepping up into the midst of victory, only to be struck down by a swarm of bullets. Such casualties feel tragic and pointless. Violence is an inescapable fact of warfare, but cheap carnage is not. There is no reason why soldiers should be cannon fodder. They ought to be given everything they need – including a formidable strategy – in order to fight with courage, intelligence, and resolve.

For me, the Battle of the Somme is a parable that reveals a sweeping tragedy within the church. Christian men today are alarmingly unprepared for spiritual warfare. By 'spiritual warfare' I am not referring to the light-saber contests between angels and demons that are imagined in cheap bestsellers. I am referencing the less titillating but far more grueling battle that each man faces daily against the lusts and sinful desires of his own heart. The memory of soldiers during WWI leaping out of trenches is a picture of the hazardous naivety of a lot of modern Christians. Every morning countless men hop out of bed with no more thought of a lethal enemy stalking them than a child eating a Mickey Mouse ice-cream bar at Disney. Men step into their cars believing that technology has made the world safe, that science has contained the most lethal of dangers, that spiritual forces like Satan and Sin are no more real or threatening than old images of Baal riding a cloud, thunderbolt in hand. The result of such naivety is that masses of men – *Christian men* – are surprised by the fierceness of the evil currents swirling in and around them. Like the unlucky soldiers at Somme, they end up being casualties of a battle they didn't fully realize was going on. *It doesn't have to be this way.*

Retracing Our Steps

How did we get here? How have so many Christian men lost sight of the dangers of the Christian life? How did the repeated warnings and admonitions of the New Testament get edited out of our contemporary worldview? There is no need here to provide an exhaustive history of the spiritual disarmament of Western Christianity. Nonetheless, three contributing factors deserve mention due to the way in which they set the stage for all that follows.

The first is the degree to which all modern people – Christian and non-Christian – are *secular*.[2] For a typical American or British male, the most important part of our schooling was not what our teachers, books, or curriculum said, but rather what was left *unsaid*. For most of us, the whole of our education, from nursery to high school, was built on one assumption: Of the many problems that jeopardize the health and happiness of the modern world, sin is not one of them. Everything from the rituals of the high street to the subject matter of history reiterated a single truth: that a person has no more reason to fear 'indwelling sin' or 'the deception of the heart' than Chicken Little had need to worry about the sky collapsing.[3]

---

2. Yuval Harari offers the terrifying insight that in the twenty-first century, religions are irrelevant because the true faith of everyone – regardless of religious preference – is defined by our technological civilization. See Yuval Harari, *21 Lessons for the 21st Century* (New York: Random House, 2018), ch. 6.

3. In a fascinating study, the American Enterprise Institute found that, in the United States, one of the most likely causes of declining religiosity is 'the increasingly intense role that more and more secularized educational institutions play in children's lives.' See https://www.aei.org/research-products/report/promise-and-peril-the-history-of-american-religiosity-and-its-recent-decline/ Accessed November 2021.

Sadly, this message has sunk in deeper than most of us care to admit. Over the last few years, I have done a lot of life-planning with men, trying to help them clarify a sense of direction and purpose in life. As part of this exercise men are asked to look at life from a variety of points of elevation in order to clarify key responsibilities and specify attainable goals. Time and again men talk about managing finances, advancing their careers, spending more time as a family, developing better habits of diet and exercise, and learning principles of focus and time-management. Yet, almost always something is missing from the list. Rare is the man who mentions mortifying sin as a part of his must-do plan. No mention is made of a need to stamp out selfish ambition, to break the back of greed, or to quench the fires of anger and lust. The problem is not that these men are not Christians or that they do not believe that sin is a legitimate threat to their overall wellbeing. The problem is that they are unconsciously steeped in a secular point of view. When it comes to *normal* thinking about *normal* life, holiness and sin, godliness and temptation drop out of the picture. Why is this? The answer is because in the modern world things like productivity and fitness feel more real and valuable than things like 'putting off the old man' or resisting the devil. The oft repeated maxim is true: All of us are a product of our education.[4]

A second contributing factor is the effect of life-management preaching. Tim Keller talks about how every sermon has not only a text and a pretext, but also a *subtext*. There is a message beneath the message which is communicated not only by the explicit words of a preacher, but also by his unconscious mannerisms, half-conceived motives, and partially mapped agendas.[5] The best way for a listener to uncover the subtext of a sermon is to ask questions like the following: 'Why are you telling me this?' 'What is the problem that you are trying to resolve?'

---

4. For insight regarding the unfelt practices that shape modern identity see Ivan Illich, *Deschooling Society* (New York: Marion Boyars, 2000).

5. Tim Keller, *Preaching: Communicating Faith in an Age of Skepticism* (New York: Penguin, 2016).

'How urgent is the solution you are sharing?' My experience is that, even in robustly evangelical churches, rare is the preacher who speaks with the earnestness and sobriety of a commanding officer instructing soldiers on the eve of a decisive battle.[6] The directness of an evangelist or prophet is swapped for the suave disposition of a life coach. This shift of tone has a slow, but formative effect upon listeners. Gradually, Christians lose the sense that they are pilgrims on a dangerous journey. Instead, they begin to view themselves as professionals, looking for life hacks or as patients needing deliverance from the greatest of all modern evils, negative emotions.

If anyone doubts the claim, a single test will demonstrate the degree to which modern preaching has lost sight of the existential threat of sin. John Owen, the greatest of English Puritans, famously said, 'Be always killing sin or sin will be killing you.'[7] A question for everyday Christians is this: When was the last time you heard a preacher make such a bold and terrifying statement regarding sin? For many, the answer is *never*. Stark biblical realism is not a defining trait of modern preaching.

Of course, one might question whether this really matters. A curious person might ask, 'What difference does it make if a preacher has a relaxed attitude regarding the danger of sin?' The problem is this: Preaching sets the thermostat for a congregation. If preachers do not see and *feel* the danger of indwelling sin, their casual attitude will be communicated to their listeners. And this is precisely what has happened in many congregations. If the man on the stage is more concerned about emotional intelligence or Enneagram scores than about sinful passions, listeners will pick up the cue. A latent secular worldview will be affirmed, and people will end up caring more

---

6. John Bunyan paints a very different portrait of the ideal preacher in *The Pilgrim's Progress*. When Christian visits the House of the Interpreter, he sees a painting of a grave man whose eyes are lifted to heaven: the Bible is in his hand, the world is behind his back, a crown hangs over his head, and he stands, pleading with men.

7. See John Owen, *The Mortification of Sin* (Kindle version).

about 'winning at work and succeeding in life' than about 'perfecting holiness in the fear of the Lord' (2 Cor. 7:1 NKJV).

Finally, a third factor deserves mention. For at least a couple of generations, a cloud of despair has dampened a general confidence in the gospel. Although few would admit it publicly, privately many share the deep anxiety that the resources of the gospel are inadequate to deal with – not the *guilt* of sin – but the *power* of sin. Even though we know that the Holy Spirit indwells us and that the hope of the gospel is that the Spirit will enable us to put sin to death, at some unidentifiable point, the mechanics of grace seem to break down for us. Can sin be forgiven? Of this we have no doubts. Can sin be defeated? Here we fidget. Reviewing a litany of experiences of repeated and persistent failure, we fumble for an answer. Old sins too often feel like nagging injuries that never go away and that cause pain and produce a handicap regardless of what measures are taken to heal them.

It is important to see how this despair influences the attitude of men toward sin. At a deep and nonconscious level, many of us choose to ignore sin because we are afraid to take an honest look at the extent of the problem. What child does not prefer to avoid a bully than to confront him? Such avoidance is characteristic of our mindset toward sin. No small portion of the effort to secularize the world is in fact an attempt to bury the pain of guilt and accountability.[8] This is true individually and collectively. Why face the reality of a heart of darkness if instead we can pretend that sin is nothing more than the shadow cast by normal human behavior?[9]

Now, if you are a Christian man holding this book, you need to ask an important question: How have I been influenced by these factors? More than likely, the problem can be summed up in a simple diagnosis:

---

8. This is a point that the philosopher Roger Scruton considers in *The Soul of the World* (Princeton: PUP, 2016).

9. The French philosopher Jean-Jacques Rousseau was one of the first to plant this dangerous seed. For a devastating critique of Rousseau, see Paul Johnson, *Intellectuals* (New York: Harper & Row, 1988), ch. 1.

No one has prepared you to fight against sin. My experience is that, when it comes to this particular battle, most Christian men are confused, frustrated, and teetering on the edge of despair. They are confused because the threadbare advice given by spiritual mentors simply does not work. None of the silver-bullet formulas like 'let go and let God' or 'rest in a new identity' have proven adequate to slay the dragons of the heart. Likewise, they are frustrated. The problem is not just that these formulas do not work; the problem is that these formulas tend to be the only advice at hand. For some inexplicable reason the following is true: Whereas studies on prayer and evangelism are a dime a dozen, a man can sit in a church for decades without ever getting in-depth training on the topic of mortifying sin. This seems to be the sticky topic that no one wants to touch. And so, where does this leave normal Christian guys? It leaves them in despair, trying to keep a grip on hope with sweaty palms. Far too many Christian men are dangerously close to swallowing the lie that following Jesus is just one long experience of getting our teeth kicked in by anger, lust, and pride. *It doesn't have to be this way.*

The Defiant Hope of the New Testament

As Christians, we can never measure our potential by our experience. Past failure is never an accurate gauge for future progress. The reason for this is because the strength of the Christian life is found in Christ, not the self. In this respect, a disciple of Christ is like a sailboat, not a speedboat. Our power is not determined by the horsepower we contain internally, but by a force that is above and beyond us, one which can fill our sails at any moment with unexpected strength and vigor.

This boundless supply of grace explains the cheerful and insistent optimism that rings throughout the New Testament. Repeatedly, Jesus and the apostles declare that sin is not our master. They lift our chin to the fact that the power of God at work in us is not just a smidge greater than the power of loitering sin. The difference between the two is the difference between a hand that flings stars into the universe and the grip of a newborn infant. Sin may look like an insurmountable problem when measured by the stature of a fallen man, but to God, sin is no more than a weed planted in sand. He can pluck out the most tenacious of habits with the ease of a child picking daisies.

Much more will be said in what follows about the mechanics of working with God to put off sin. In no way do I want to suggest here that the process of killing sin will be painless or easy. However, our first need is not to summon courage, but to banish despair. As we read the New Testament, we ought to be shocked by how natural it is for Paul and other New Testament writers to talk about sin being resisted, put off, and *slain*. In Colossians 3:5, Paul tells us to kill sin with the matter-of-factness of a supervisor telling workers to go out into the backyard and trim the hedges. His confidence that such work is actually possible is astounding when compared to the attitudes of modern Christians. Nothing in Paul's epistles suggests that such work is a Herculean task reserved for the spiritual commandos among us. In Paul's mind, normal Christians going about normal lives have the ability, indeed responsibility, to 'put to death the deeds of the body' (Rom. 8:13).

The same tone of confidence is heard in the voice of Jesus. In John's gospel, Jesus says, 'Truly, truly, I say to you, everyone who practices sin is a slave of sin. The slave does not remain in the house forever; the son remains forever. So if the Son sets you free, you will be free indeed' (8:34-36). No follower of Christ can read these words and justify a defeatist attitude regarding sin. The freedom that Christ unfurls is not a reward granted to the meritorious, but the free gift of Christ Himself: *If the Son makes you free.* There is no way to read the Gospel of John or any other New Testament book and avoid the following truth: The death and resurrection of Jesus was not an act of resistance against sin, but a definitive victory over sin. This means that to be united with Christ is to be named among *victors*. We are 'more than conquerors through him who loved us' (Rom. 8:37). Such words ought to do for us what the severed head of Goliath did for the trembling hearts of the Israelites. We ought to feel our spine tingle and our fists tighten as we shake off the chills of cowardice and leap into the fray against the remnants of sin.

Defining Success

There is nothing worse than overpromising and under-delivering. A lot of contemporary books follow the blueprint of infomercials. I'll never forget an advertisement for the 'ab-roller' that aired when I was in high school. One moment you would see images of pear-shaped Americans. The next, the camera would turn to images of men and women who looked like Zeus and Hera doing crunches with a simple sit-up machine. The message was clear. If a person was willing to spend just five minutes a day doing crunches with a magic device, a miracle would occur: in a few months he would be transformed from Chris Farley into Chris Hemsworth (aka Thor).

Such wishful thinking needs to be swatted away like a fly buzzing around the head. This book will not provide a quick, instant, and eternal cure for all sin and temptation. Anyone who promises snake oil ought to be recognized for what he is, a huckster. Sin is no small obstacle. With sin we are talking about a force so great and deadly that the Son of God had to be nailed to a tree in order for its rule to be broken. That fact alone ought to be sufficient to convince us that vanquishing the lingering strongholds of sin will be a long and tiring task.

So, then, what does this book offer? How will a man benefit from reading it? The best way to answer the question is by recalling a scene from John Bunyan's classic work, *The Pilgrim's Progress*.

In this scene, Christian, the main character, visits a large mansion called Palace Beautiful. The reader might think that Christian was nearing the end of his pilgrimage when he arrives at the palace. After all, by the time he reaches the house, he has nearly suffocated in a miry pit, almost had rocks crush his head, been targeted by deadly arrows, and had to retrace his steps – in the dark – on a steep hill called 'Difficulty.' The reader can't help but wonder, how much worse can things get before the journey is over? The answer is *a lot*. Still lying ahead of Christian is a fierce duel with Apollyon, near martyrdom at Vanity Fair, brutal torture in the dungeon of Doubting Castle, and a laundry list of lesser trials. Given this painful itinerary, we can see that the location of Palace Beautiful in the story is not accidental. It marks a key moment of growth when Christian takes another step toward becoming a mature and seasoned pilgrim.

Now several things happen to Christian during his stay at the palace. He is given a luxurious room in which to sleep and rest. The clouds clear for a moment so that he can catch a glimpse of Immanuel's Land, his final destination. He is even shown relics of famous battles, where saints of old triumphed in the most distressing of circumstances. Yet, the part of relevance to us is the moment when Christian is finally given armor to wear for the remainder of his journey. He is handed a helmet, shield, sword, breastplate, and shoes to protect him from the perils ahead. Pausing for a moment, we need to take note of the significance of Christian being given this protective gear. It is not normal to be given body armor when you spend the night at a bed and breakfast. Why, then, of all the gifts that Christian might receive, is he given weapons?

These gifts hint at several important truths. They are a telltale sign that there are no shortcuts for the journey ahead. They eliminate any hope that there are secret techniques to ease, or by-pass, encroaching battles. They dash any latent wish that Christian can sit comfortably at the palace and wait for Immanuel Himself to arrive in a golden chariot. The message of having to put on armor is plain: Christian must continue to travel down a difficult and dangerous road if he is to reach the Celestial City. He must be ready for war.

And so, as Christian departs from the palace, a small but notable change has happened to him. He has not turned into John Rambo overnight; however, neither is he the same as he was before. In short, the man who entered the palace a modest pilgrim exits an armed knight. A sword is now in hand. He is prepared for combat.

The silhouette of a pilgrim holding a sword is a perfect image of what this book can do for the reader. There is an old tradition of writing an *enchiridion* of the Christian faith. This strange, Greek word originally referred to a short sword that was light and easy to wield. When such towering figures as St. Augustine or Erasmus set out to write an *enchiridion*, they were signaling a desire to offer readers something more akin to a helpful tool than a hefty tome. They understood that a book can be a weapon if presented in the right way.

This book is written in the same spirit. No brittle solutions will be offered for complex problems. All shortcuts will be rejected with sober disdain. This book has been written with one objective in mind: to equip ordinary Christian men for the long road of fighting evil passions, which is the road that Christ has called all of us to follow.[10]

An Overview of the Journey Ahead

It is always helpful to glance at a road map before beginning a journey. Here is a quick overview of the itinerary ahead.

The first chapter will consider ten basic rules of war. A lot of us have picked up unhelpful assumptions about what it means to fight sin. The focus of this chapter will be to correct the background knowledge that we carry with us into the battle against sin.

The second chapter will focus on detecting the propaganda of sin. We tend to think of the fight against sin as primarily a contest that involves the will. We either consent to a temptation or reject it. However, much of the battle against sin is a cold war, not a hot one. Long before any particular temptation arises, there is a hidden battle between truth and deceit. If men desire to resist sinful desire, they need first to develop the habit of detecting and rejecting lies. This chapter will show men how to cultivate a vigilant mind.

The theme of the third chapter is killing entrenched passions. All of us know what it is like to have an idol lodged in the heart. Under

---

10. It is worth mentioning that shortly after Christian leaves the Palace Beautiful, he comes upon a companion named Faithful. Here Bunyan is reminding us of a point that will need to be kept in mind throughout this book, namely, that fighting sin should never be a solitary task. We fight better when we fight together. For more on spiritual friendship see Joe Barnard, *The Way Forward: a Road Map of Spiritual Growth for Men in the 21st Century* (Fearn: Christian Focus Publications, 2019), pp. 87-95.

these circumstances we feel as if we are under a kind of magic spell. Like Eve, we choose the forbidden fruit because our vision is skewed. What should appear evil instead looks good. How does a man go about adjusting his vision? This is the difficult question that will be answered in this chapter.

In the last chapter, we narrow the focus by targeting four particular sins that are wreaking havoc in the lives of modern men. Two of these are well known, pride and lust. The other two are more obscure, but no less dangerous, vanity and sloth. All four need to be diligently fought if a man desires to make progress in a life of godliness.

A final word: In the Royal Navy there is a saying: *si vis pacem, para bellum* ('If you want peace, prepare for war'). These words cut to the heart of this book. Too many men are pursuing peace through a life of spiritual apathy. No more dangerous path could be chosen. Avoidance will never deter the aggression of the enemy. We either fight or we surrender. This book is for men who are willing to fight.

1

The Rules of War

◁◁◁♦♦♦▷▷▷

Let's go back to 1916. The Battle of Somme is festering like an infected wound. You are a young British soldier who has just arrived at the battlefield in order to replace the most recent wave of casualities. As you step into the trenches for the first time, dread clinches your gut in a tight knot. You imagine the gore of bayonet combat. You watch as rats scurry in and out holes beside your feet. The acrid smell of sweat and decay leaves a tang of stomach acid in your mouth.

Passing a bunk room, you notice a veteran soldier sitting on his helmet. Like a magnet, you are drawn to him. You squat beside him, tap his shoulder, and – without any introduction – you ask, *'What do I need to know? How does a man survive here?'*

Such urgency is the starting line of this chapter. Too often spiritual books are written either with the relaxed tone of a travel guide or the emotional detachment of a professor writing on the mating habits of earthworms. This spirit may be okay if the topic is building friendships or leading small groups. However, if the subject matter is sin, such tones are absurd. Sin can never be a mere talking point. Its fangs are too near and its bite too deadly to permit a relaxed and comfortable attitude. In truth, the only way to talk about sin is with a touch of nervousness. No man feels completely at ease while chatting to his doctor about prostate cancer. How, then, can we discuss pride or lust without hearing the rustling of a predator crouching at the door?

The purpose of this chapter is to lay down ten basic ground rules for warring against sin. Sin is a unique opponent. One of the greatest threats in our fight against sin is the assumption that competence in the world qualifies us to handle sin. It doesn't. We cannot transpose, for example, life-management skills into tactics for mortifying the flesh. Many a preacher has likened sin to a pig that will eat anything set before it. We need to be careful lest our efforts at self-improvement end up engorging the very flesh we are trying to starve.

All that is written here should be read as the notes of one soldier being passed to another. I will be brief. I will be frank. Now is not the time to shave fine hairs of doctrine while sipping a single malt. The smell of battle is in the air. Our focus needs to be on essential intelligence, the kind of information Christian men need *right now* in order to resist malignant forces that are already scheming their downfall.

One last thing needs to be said by way of introduction. Each of these rules is built on a verse from Paul's letter to the Romans. The reason for this is as follows: Romans is Paul's most lengthy, complete, and systematic presentation of the gospel. This gospel – the core message of the death and resurrection of Jesus Christ – is the only remedy for sin. Thus, if a man is looking for a training manual for how to put sin to death, there is no better place to go than Romans.

Rule 1 – You Need the Holy Spirit

'For the law of the Spirit of Life has set you free in Christ Jesus from the law of sin and death' (Rom. 8:2).

Humility could be the most misunderstood virtue of the Christian life. Culturally, we tend to think of a humble person as someone who is timid, insecure, and self-demeaning. He is the perfect Bob Cratchit

– the drone in a cubicle who is willing to sacrifice life, liberty, and all personal happiness in order to keep his line manager, Mr. Scrooge, happy. Yet, true humility is as different from this caricature as a lion is from a house cat. The distinguishing mark of genuine humility is not a correct posture of me-before-me, or of me-before-my-boss, but of me-before-God. Humility is a purebred theological virtue. Only when I understand and *own* my true relationship with God am I free to be a humble man.[1]

This explains why humility is able to unite such extremes within a single human heart. On the one hand, a humble man is able to walk with the cool confidence of David into the shadow of a giant.[2] He can do so for one reason: behind the giant he sees the much larger shadow of an infinite God. At the same time, humility ensures that such confidence never trespasses into the domain of pride. The humble man understands the source of all of his strength. He knows that, if God is on his side, mountains can be tossed like pebbles into the sea. However, if left alone, a pebble is too great of a mountain to be picked up and carried.

This background is important for understanding how humility weighs into the fight against sin. There are two attitudes that threaten to handicap a Christian at every moment of this battle. One is despair, the feeling that sin is too strong of an enemy to be defeated. This disposition takes root whenever we repeat the mistake of the wandering Israelites at the border of Canaan. If we focus on the stature of our enemy instead of the stature of God, all perspective is lost and we end up feeling like mice, not men. The other equally treacherous attitude is

---

1. Two books worth reading on humility are the following: the classic *Humility* by Andrew Murray (multiple digital versions available) and the more recent book by C. J. Mahaney, *Humility: True Greatness* (Colorado Springs: Multnomah Books, 2005).

2. Note the stanza in Frederick Faber's old hymn 'Workman of God': 'Thrice blessed is he to whom is given/The instinct that can tell/That God is on the field/ when He is most invisible.'

that of pride, the deep-seated feeling that I-can-get-on-without-God. This attitude would be comic if it were not so dangerous. Any man who tries to face sin armed merely with the flesh will undoubtedly wind up like the Israelites outside the gates of Ai – whipped and licking his wounds.[3]

Now to maintain humility in the fight against sin we need to understand what Paul says in Romans 8:2: 'For the law of the Spirit of life has set you free in Christ Jesus from the law of sin and death.'[4] The idea here is that, when a person becomes a Christian, he experiences a change of regimes. An old tyrant is deposed. A new order is established. We might liken this to the fate of Paris during WW2. Early in 1940 Paris fell to the Nazis. However, on the 25th of August, 1944, after a six-day battle, the German garrison finally surrendered. For people on the ground, this meant that there was a radical shift of authority within the city. One day, the Nazi commanders were telling citizens what they could and could not do. The next, they were stripped of power. The Allies were now in control.

Such is the nature of conversion. Christ does not just save people from the penalty of sin. He liberates them from the dominion of sin. This is what Paul is telling us in Romans 8:2. He wants us to know that, in place of sin and death, Christ now rules in the hearts of His people through the presence and power of the Holy Spirit.

Now there are two principles that follow this truth. They are two sides of the same coin. The first is that, apart from the Spirit, no one can fight sin, much less kill sin. Without the might of God at work in us, the most we will ever be able to do against sin is echo the cry of

---

3. Our dependence on the Spirit is a point that John Owen hammers home in *The Mortification of Sin*. He says, 'A man may easier see without eyes, speak without a tongue, than truly mortify one sin without the Spirit.'

4. We need to not be confused by Paul's use of law here. What he means by the term is not a set of rules, but a source of power, authority, and control. See Douglas Moo, *The Letter to the Romans* (Grand Rapids: Eerdmans, 2018), p. 493.

Romans 7: 'Wretched man that I am! Who will deliver me from this body of death?' (v. 24)⁵

Yet, the flip side is also true. If without the Spirit, nothing is possible, with the Spirit, all things are possible. The same Spirit who enabled Samson to hoist the city gates and topple pagan temples now lives within us. Understanding this is the key to genuine humility. Humility is the posture that enables us to say, 'When I am weak, then I am strong.' When humble, we are both empty and full. We are emptied of self-confidence, but brimming with hope in the strength of the Lord. This attitude is the starting position of all effective combat against sin.⁶

Rule 2 – You Need to Know Your Location

'So you also must consider yourselves dead to sin and alive to God in Christ Jesus' (Rom. 6:11).

The New Testament often uses the image of being awakened to describe the lived experience of faith. To be unconverted is not just to sit in darkness; it is to be asleep. The unbelieving man is spiritually detached from reality. He is living in delusion, unaware of truths that ought to have a greater impact on his life than the ground beneath his feet, the sun in the sky, and the air that he breathes.

Now, it is a strange experience to be awakened from a deep sleep, especially if one has radically changed locations. I'll never forget traveling to Egypt to study as a young man. I arrived late at night after a full day of flying. A family picked me up that I had never met before. I was taken to their apartment and brought to a bedroom where I

---

5. We can neatly sum this truth up in the formula: no regeneration, no mortification.

6. Many a spiritual writer has made the point that, while humility is not the highest virtue, it is the first virtue. It is a unique beauty that attracts the mercy of God. Bernard of Clairvaux writes, 'And so when you perceive that you are being humiliated, look on it as a sign of a sure guarantee that grace is on the way.' See *Sermons on the Song of Songs* (Kindle edition).

would be staying for the next couple of weeks. Jet-lagged and delirious, I stumbled into bed.

The next day I woke up in the early afternoon. I didn't know what time it was, where I was staying, or anything about the world around me. I remember looking through the window and seeing sandy lawns and palm trees. I felt as if I was standing at the intersection of two worlds, one old and familiar and one new and unknown.

The situation of Christians is similar to this. After coming to faith, our bodies continue to inhabit the same physical world that we have known from birth. And yet after hearing the gospel something is startlingly new. A light has shone on our hearts that makes truths evident that previously we could not perceive, imagine, or understand. Like newborn infants, we are thrown into dimensions of existence that are as new and unfamiliar as they are exciting and unexpected.

In light of this dramatic change, one of the primary responsibilities of every Christian is to reorient himself using the fixed truths of the gospel.[7] This is what Paul means when he says, 'So you also must consider yourselves dead to sin and alive to God in Christ Jesus' (Rom. 6:11). For Paul, the gospel is not a set of religious ideas suspended from reality like clouds in the sky. The gospel is a statement of historical facts. This means that, for Paul, learning about the gospel is a lot like reading a topographical map. The gospel orients us. It tells us where we've come from, where we are going, where we are located right now, and in which direction we need to get moving.

Now, for killing sin, nothing is more important than getting an accurate read on where we are situated before God. One of Satan's favorite tactics is to convince us that we are walking on the boggy

---

7. It's increasingly common to reduce our union with Christ to the language of identity. There is a danger in this trend. To modern ears, the idea of 'identity' is muddled with subjective, individualistic, and psychological overtones. For a more robust treatment of union with Christ see Douglas Moo, *The Letter to the Romans*, pp. 378-422.

ground of condemnation and guilt when in fact we are standing on the solid rock of grace and forgiveness. Satan constantly sends out mixed signals to try to confuse us about our status in Christ. The best defense for this is to pull out our map of the gospel and to remind ourselves of our location. We need to look back and remember that, when Christ died, we died. This means there is no more condemnation for us. Equally, we need to look ahead and see that, if Christ was raised, then we, too, will be raised. This means that there is no more despair for us. Thus, being reminded of our position before God, we can journey on in confidence having shed the dead weight of confusion, doubt, shame, and guilt.[8]

Rule 3 – You Need to Practice the Normal Christian Life
'Do not be slothful in zeal' (Rom. 12:11).

As I write we are in the middle of a pandemic. One of the dangers during a crisis is to succumb to tunnel vision. Right now, hundreds of billions of dollars have been invested in the effort to develop a vaccine to subdue the spread of Covid-19. There is a widespread feeling that if we can just manage this particular virus then the world can safely return to normality.

Though the vaccine effort is commendable, the mindset is short-sighted. Covid has undoubtedly exacerbated the health risks of millions of people. Nonetheless, the idea that sustaining health can be reduced to inoculating against a single virus is distressingly naïve. To state the obvious, safeguarding health requires a lot more than medical intervention. It requires regular exercise, a disciplined diet, abstaining from harmful substances, getting sufficient sleep, and even maintaining meaningful relationships. As necessary as a vaccine may be for reducing the danger of a specific virus, the

---

8. For a good introduction to the gospel, see Jerry Bridges, *Transforming Grace* (Colorado Springs: NavPress, 2017).

routine practices of everyday life are far more important in terms of sustaining the robust organs and vigorous immune system needed to keep the body healthy.

A similar risk endangers our effort against sin. There is a bizarre aspect of human nature that prefers the exciting and exceptional to the routine and ordinary. Lewis captures this in *The Screwtape Letters*. In the book, an elder demon is coaching a protégé in how to disrupt the religious awakening of a man. The elder demon writes,

> Keep his mind off the most elementary duties by directing it to the most advanced and spiritual ones. Aggravate that most useful human characteristic, the horror and neglect of the obvious. You must bring him to a condition in which he can practice self-examination for an hour without discovering any of those facts about himself which are perfectly clear to anyone who has ever lived in the same house with him or worked in the same office.[9]

This bias to neglect the obvious is a genuine danger in spiritual combat. When it comes to fighting sin, many of us would prefer to do something unusual and dramatic – like joining Tony Robbins in a bout of firewalking – than cycling through a humble routine of church services, Bible reading, and prayer. The stuff of everyday discipleship sounds boring, repetitive, and ritualistic. Thus, we gravitate toward the novel and adventurous.

This aversion to the normal Christian life is exceedingly dangerous. Killing sin always begins with the mundane, not the extraordinary. If a man wants to snuff the coals of lust or anger, the first step is not a silent retreat, but something far simpler: sitting under a faithful ministry of the Word, committing to a local fellowship, budgeting time for spiritual friendship and communal worship, and establishing personal routines of Word and prayer. More can always be added to

---

9. C. S. Lewis, *The Screwtape Letters* (New York: Harpers Collins, 2011), p. 19.

this recipe, but these ingredients can never be taken away. They are as basic to killing sin as flour and water are for making bread.[10]

Why is this? A lot of reasons could be given. I will just refer to one. The normal Christian life is what produces and sustains the basic health of a Christian. In saying this I am not denying that more aggressive efforts will be needed to dig up the roots of some gnarly sins. The point is merely that pursuing a silver-bullet cure will be of little benefit to a person who is not first willing to practice the A, B, C's of a godly lifestyle.

Rule 4 – You Need a Zero-Tolerance Attitude

'If you live according to the flesh you will die, but if by the Spirit you put to death the deeds of the body, you will live' (Rom. 8:13).

We all live with a mental scale of illnesses. At one end of the spectrum, there are various ailments that are not alarming. For most people catching a cold is an annual rite of passage. They lose no sleep when they get a stuffy nose or a touch of fever. Then there is the other end of the spectrum, the scary diseases that we avoid thinking too much about. At the top of this list are maladies like cancer and dementia. The average person would do anything possible to keep himself from experiencing one of these. We fear them like we fear death itself – and for good reason: the one all too easily leads to the other.

Christians often have a similar mentality regarding sin. There are small sins, and there are big sins. The former do not worry us. We imagine that a touch of greed or a critical spirit will gently evaporate with time like water on a towel. The stuff that scares us are the big sins

---

10. Men need to realize that we have a spiritual shadow just as we have a physical one. Our shadow is the part of us that we do not want to see and that we deny being in existence. There is no way to mortify sin without confronting our shadow. Yet, how do we do this? The best way to come to terms with the dark side of our person is not self-examination, but living in close relationships with other people. What is invisible to 'me' will be clear to 'you.'

– murder, adultery, theft, abuse, and so on. These, we imagine, are the hard felonies that imprison the soul.[11]

When applied to sin, the idea of a spectrum is perversely unhelpful. Sin is not like an assortment of diseases, some worse than others. If we want an accurate picture of sin, we need to think of something like cancer, which is a single disease that produces a host of different symptoms. In fact, the likeness between sin and cancer is uncanny. In a book on the body, Bill Bryson writes,

> Cancer is quite unlike other maladies. It is often relentless in its attacks. Victory against it is nearly always hard won and often at great cost to the victim's overall health. It will retreat under an onslaught, regroup, and return in a more potent form. Even when seemingly defeated, it may leave behind 'sleeper' cells that can lie dormant for years before springing to life again. Above all, cancer cells are selfish. Normally, human cells do their job, then die on command when instructed by other cells for the good of the body. Cancer cells don't. They proliferate entirely in their own interests.[12]

He later adds, 'Most cancers in their early stages are painless and invisible. It is only when tumors grow big enough to press on nerves or form a lump that we become aware that something is wrong.'

We could rewrite these exact sentences replacing the word 'cancer' with 'sin.' All of the sinister traits of the one are true of the other. Sin is always moving in the heart. If resisted in one area, sin is quick to retreat, regroup, and shift elsewhere in the effort to go undetected until sufficiently strong. Once we realize this, we can understand why treating some sins as if they are 'minor' and others as 'major' is hazardous. Sin, like cancer, only ever has one trajectory – the death of

---

11. For treatment of the so-called 'minor sins,' see Jerry Bridges *Respectable Sins* (Colorado Springs: NavPress, 2017).
12. See Bill Bryson, *The Body: a Guide for Occupants* (New York: Anchor, 2019), p. 337.

a person. How sin kills is a moot point. It is as content for a host to die by gossip or stinginess as by brutality and cruelty.

Two principles flow from this important truth. The first is this: *The only way to fight any one sin is to fight all sin.* What good does it do if a doctor treats cancer in the bladder but does nothing to eliminate malignant cells in the prostate or the lungs? To leave the disease to fester in any one place is to surrender further ground in the near future. The same is true with sin. Allow a foothold of pride and anger will spring to life. Indulge lust and greed will grow. Permit envy to take root and malice will spread.[13]

This leads to a second principle: *The only way to fight big sins is to fight small ones.* Sin always snowballs. One lie leads to two lies, which leads to four, which leads to sixteen. Before a man can come to his senses, he is tumbling recklessly through life in a giant avalanche of deceit. This means that no temptation can be viewed in isolation. Sin never leads to a cul de sac. A person is never simply choosing a single action. He is always choosing a long-term trajectory.[14]

Rule 5 – You Need to Be All-In

'Present your bodies as a living sacrifice holy and acceptable to God' (Rom. 12:1).

When most guys think about killing sin – if they think about it at all – they imagine a limited activity, something akin to a morning workout or doing an occasional performance review at work. As long as the pit

---

13. John Owen says, 'If we will do anything, we must do all things. So, then, it is not only an intense opposition to this or that peculiar lust, but a universal humble frame and temper of heart, with watchfulness over every evil and for the performance of every duty, that is accepted.' See *The Mortification of Sin* (Kindle version).

14. The following remark by the elder demon in *The Screwtape Letters* should be kept in mind: 'Indeed the safest road to Hell is the gradual one – the gentle slope, soft underfoot, without sudden turnings, without milestones, without signposts.' See C. S. Lewis, *The Screwtape Letters*, p. 57.

of addiction is avoided, the thought never occurs to them that a more holistic, full-bodied strategy is required. Such naivety is why so many men see so little freedom from sin. In truth, there is no such thing as part-time mortification. You are either all-in, or the little effort you expend will be of no avail.

Paul makes this clear in Romans 12:1. It is interesting that he does not say 'present your minds,' or 'present your hearts,' or 'present your spirits' as a living sacrifice. Instead, he says 'present your bodies.' Just about any other word that he might have used in place of 'body' would have created a divide between an inner realm and an outer realm, or between a spiritual realm and a secular realm. Yet, the mention of 'body' erases all of these distinctions. For Paul, the world is not made up of spiritual places like the church and secular places like the gym. There are not holy activities like prayer and Bible reading and profane activities like grocery shopping and commuting. In Paul's thinking, wherever the body is, that is where discipleship happens. A person is either pursuing Christ everywhere or else he is a gross caricature of the Christian life.[15]

This general principle of discipleship is important for fighting sin. As soon as life is compartmentalized, we end up tolerating attitudes and behavior in one segment of life that we would never permit in another. It becomes okay to talk about women at a locker room in a manner that would be shameful at a Bible study. Such inconsistency needs to be labeled for what it is, *hypocrisy*.[16]

Mortification cannot be reduced to adapting to different sets of rules in different social settings. Such is the game of hiding sin, not

---

15. A very helpful book that shows the role of the body in discipleship is Dallas Willard's *The Spirit of the Disciplines: Understanding How God Changes Lives* (San Francisco: Harper, 1999), pp. 75-95.
16. In Luke 12:1-3 Jesus says, 'Beware of the leaven of the Pharisees, which is hypocrisy. Nothing is covered up that will not be revealed, or hidden that will not be known. Therefore whatever you have said in the dark shall be heard in the light, and what you have whispered in private rooms shall be proclaimed on the housetops.'

killing it. If a man is earnest in his desire to mortify sin, then he needs to accept the following rule: You either kill sin everywhere, or you kill sin nowhere. Our theater of war is not part of life, but the whole of life.[17]

Rule 6 – You Need to Play Strong Defense

'Let not sin therefore reign in your mortal body, to make you obey its passions' (Rom. 6:12).

When children are abused, there is a terrible phenomenon called disassociation. They mentally detach from reality for as long as the painful experience is happening. Only after the deed is finished, do they re-enter normal consciousness and resume control of themselves.

Often, in moments of temptation, we do the same. We sit back and become passive as the winds of coveting or selfishness begin to blow. For as long as they are present, we let them have their way. Minimal effort is put forth to subdue or resist them.

For children suffering harm, this mechanism makes sense. They are powerless to do anything about the trauma they are experiencing. However, this is not the condition of Christians with respect to sin. No sin has any right over us. Its power is only by permission. It is only if we allow sin to be our master that we find ourselves doing its bidding.

This is Paul's point in Romans 6:12. Up until this verse, Paul has been explaining the significance of our union with Christ. He has pushed hard the point that, if Christ died, then we have died; if Christ is alive, then we are alive – not just physically – but spiritually. In verse 12 he then takes this teaching and applies it. He tells us that our freedom from sin is not something that happens mechanically. If we want to enjoy liberty, we need to put up resistance. It is only if we are willing to say *'No!'* to sin that the momentum of sin begins to stall.

---

17. Jerry Bridges says, 'There must be an attitude of diligent obedience in every area if we are to succeed in mortifying any one expression of sin.' See Jerry Bridges, *The Pursuit of Holiness* (Colorado Springs: NavPress, 2016), ch. 11.

It is important to recognize just how countercultural Paul's teaching on this point is – both within the church and outside of it. First, looking beyond the walls of the church, we increasingly live in a world that tells us that fulfillment and authenticity are the product of being true to oneself.[18] Among other things, this is a message that inner passions are not something to question and filter, but something to heed and obey. Christians too often are influenced by this message. It is not unusual to hear a Christian explain that his motive for sexual immorality is nothing more than, 'It makes me happy.' Anyone who reads the New Testament ought to be shocked by such statements. The Bible is clear that passion is a lot like crude oil. It must be strained and purified before being combusted in the heart. And even then, some passions must be altogether rejected. This is why Peter says, 'Beloved, I urge you as sojourners and exiles to abstain from the passions of the flesh, which wage war against your soul' (1 Pet. 2:11).

Yet, this idea of forcefully resisting sin is also countercultural within the church. Too many modern pastors are hypersensitive about saying anything that might suggest that Christians need to exert effort in their spiritual lives. There is no end of sermons right now that talk as if sin will magically dissolve if a person can just catch sight of the beauty of Jesus. *If only our hearts were as simple as this.* The honest truth, which we all know from experience, is that the heart is notoriously inconsistent. Like a bell it swings from the ding of praising God to the dong of courting sin – back and forth, back and forth.[19]

Fortunately, Paul is more honest than a lot of pastors when it comes to addressing the fickleness of the heart. He is unequivocal: If we want

---

[18]. No one has diagnosed this condition more accurately than Charles Taylor. See *The Ethics of Authenticity* (Cambridge: HUP, 2018).

[19]. Regarding the fickleness of the human heart, John Newton writes, 'The exceeding sinfulness of sin is manifested, not so much by its breaking through the restraint of threatenings and commands, as by its being capable of acting against light and against love.' From 'Grace in the Ear', *Letters of John Newton*.

sin to die, then we need to put up a defensive stand.[20] This may be hard. It may take effort. Often it is only after years of slipping into pits of sinful habits that finally we hit rock bottom and cry out, 'Enough!' Yet, the fact that we are exerting effort should not discourage us. It is a sign of strength, not of weakness – a sign that the Spirit of God is within us, actively working to oppose the forces of sin.[21]

Rule 7 – You Need to Play Even Stronger Offense

'Present yourselves to God as those who have been brought from death to life, and your members to God as instruments for righteousness' (Rom. 6:13).

Defense is good, but defense is not enough. In the 2020 Super Bowl, the Kansas City Chiefs were playing the San Francisco 49ers. Kansas City was an offensive powerhouse. Blink at the wrong moment and you would miss a touchdown. San Francisco was an old school football team. They played tough defense, drained the clock, and methodically suffocated their opponent like a python with its prey.

Now, midway through the game San Francisco was winning. Yet, at halftime I remember saying to a friend, 'San Francisco is going to lose.' The problem was that they were not being aggressive on offense. They were content to try to control the game with a paper-thin lead.

---

20. It is useful here to recall J. I. Packer's statement, 'Holiness teaching that skips over disciplined persistence in the well-doing that forms holy habits is thus weak; habit forming is the Spirit's ordinary way of leading us on in holiness.' See J. I. Packer, *Keep in Step with the Spirit* (Old Tappan: Fleming H. Revell, 1983), pp. 108-9.

21. John Owen describes the way in which the Holy Spirit works in and through us as follows: 'He doth not so work our mortification in us as not to keep it still an act of our *obedience*. The Holy Ghost works in us and upon us, as we are fit to be wrought in and upon; that is, so as to preserve our own liberty and free obedience. He works upon our understandings, wills, consciences, and affections, agreeably to their own natures; he works *in us* and *with us,* not *against us* or *without us*; so that his assistance is an encouragement as to the facilitating of the work, and no occasion of neglect as to the work itself.' See *The Mortification of Sin* (Kindle version).

Sure enough, San Francisco ended up losing the game. A few minutes in the final quarter was all that Kansas City needed to turn the tide and win the championship.

To fight sin, men need to avoid the mistake of San Francisco. Too often we limit our tactics against sin to defensive measures. We give little thought to avoiding known temptation; we counter the first movements of evil passion; we even take stock of known vices and attempt to resist them. All of this is good; however, it is not enough. Defense *alone* will never smother the life of sin. Unless we are pursuing holiness, avoiding sinfulness will be of little use.[22]

In practice, this means two things. First, it means that men must exert as much effort into putting on virtue as they do in putting off vice. There is a very old saying that nature abhors a vacuum. This is as true of the soul as it is of the universe. No one can simply pluck out a sin like lust. This would leave an empty space in the heart. Instead, for sin to be removed, it must be replaced. A sin like lust will only be diminished if and when purity begins to grow in the heart.[23]

A second application is of equal importance. For virtue to grow, all of the members and faculties of our personhood must be involved. In Romans 6:13 Paul tells us to present our members as instruments of righteousness. We need to pause for a moment and consider what he means by members. Members is not referring merely to eyes, ears, arms, and legs. Paul is using the term to refer to all of the faculties

---

22. Richard Livingstone makes the following astute observation: 'One is apt to think of moral failure as due to weakness in character: more often it is due to an inadequate ideal. We detect in others, and occasionally in ourselves, the want of courage, of industry, of persistence, which leads to defeat. But we do not notice the more subtle and disastrous weaknesses, that our standards are wrong, that we have never learned what is good.' See Richard Livingston, *On Education: the Future in Education and Education in a World Adrift* (Cambridge: CUP, 1954) p. 158.

23. Evidence of this is the fact that Paul never talks about putting off *without* very quickly moving on to speaking of putting on cf. Col. 3:5, 7, 10, 12.

that give us a *personal existence*. Mind, imagination, will, memory, emotion, conscience, body – all of these are included.[24] Paul is telling us that every single one of these members must be sharpened and wielded as a weapon if we hope to live a life of holiness before God.

For a lot of men this will be a novel thought. Many of us are passive when it comes to something like the imagination. We think that our mind drifts according to uncontrollable forces. We never pause to think that the books we read (or don't read), or the movies we watch (or don't watch), or the media platforms we pay attention to (or don't pay attention to) might influence the direction of our drifting thought life. We never stop to think that we ought to expend at least as much effort maintaining our imaginations as we spend maintaining our cars and homes.[25]

The same could be said of all the other faculties listed above. Every soldier knows that maintaining his weapons is vital for combat. We need the same mindset. Much of the battle will be determined by the precondition of our mind, will, conscience, and deep affections. To neglect these is like forgetting to clean a gun or to sharpen a knife. No Christian should make such a rookie mistake.

Rule 8 – You Need to Be Radical

'Make no provision for the flesh, to gratify its desires' (Rom. 13:14).

Human beings are governed by a status quo bias. We do not like to change. We do not like to admit we are wrong. Therefore, when fighting sin, we tend to do the absolute minimum that we think will be required in order to put away our sinful passions. Jesus understood this bias, which is one reason why He used such extreme language when talking

---

24. See Douglas Moo, *Paul's Letter to the Romans*, pp. 384-5.
25. Thomas Chalmers is particularly useful in showing the way in which our use of attention directs our emotions and consequently makes us morally responsible for our emotional lives. See Thomas Chalmers, *On the Power, Wisdom, and Goodness of God*, ch. 4 (digital copies available).

about sin (cf. Matt. 5:29-30). He knew that we needed to be shocked out of our complacency. The typical human response is that, if my eye causes me to stumble, I ignore the twinge of guilt and look anyway. If my hand finds its way into the cookie jar (yet again!), I blank my conscience and grab two instead of one. Sinful people are remarkably adept at setting up routines and environments that reinforce their failure. Even though we know that we struggle with lust, we buy smartphones and subscribe to HULU anyway. Even though we know that Facebook and Instagram promote status-anxiety and envy, we nonetheless refuse to go to sleep until we have swiped our feeds one last time. Such tomfoolery needs to be contested if we are serious about killing sin. Sin is a radical problem. The only way to remove it is through radical action.

Now, by saying that men need to be radical, I mean two things. The first is that, if we desire to fight sin, we must be willing to make fundamental changes to our environment, daily habits, and lifestyle.[26] In Romans 13:14 Paul says, 'Make no provision for the flesh, to gratify its desires.' The idea is that there should be no forethought, or allowance, for sin. Modern Christians need to take this exhortation to heart. For some reason the only time Christians seem to think that drastic change is required to mortify the flesh is in the wake of sexual misconduct or unrelenting addiction. The following anomaly is clear proof of this. When it comes to pornography, there are any number of books that counsel men to cut the cable lines and sign up for accountability software. Some books even go so far as to advise men to hand over their car keys to a friend.[27] Yet, while there is a stack of such books on the topic of pornography, no similar books are available on the topics

---

26. There is no denying the relationship between environments, triggers, and habituated actions. On these connections, see Charles Duhigg, *The Power of Habit: Why We Do What We Do in Life and Business* (New York: Random House, 2014), pp. 3-31.

27. See Heath Lambert, *Finally Free: Fighting for Purity with the Power of Grace* (Grand Rapids: Zondervan, 2013), ch. 4.

of vanity, slothfulness, or selfish ambition. Why is this? The answer is certainly not because pornography is the only danger that threatens men. The answer is because Christian men (and Christian leaders) are content with some sins and not with others. Such complacency must be shaken off. Men must realize that radical change is not just required for some sin; radical change is required for all sin. If we are not willing to cut off obvious supply lines to evil passions, then we cannot expect the strength of these passions to be diminished over time.[28]

But killing sin requires being radical in a second way. The word radical comes from the Latin 'radix,' which means 'root.' This reminds us that if we want to deal with the heart of sin we need to go to the heart of the problem. Now, this topic could be explored in several different ways. I want to feature one truth that needs to be made clear in any book on the topic of fighting sin. We often think of sin as being driven entirely by a nearsighted desire for pleasure. Yet, this is not the case. Sin is as happy to feast on pain as it is on pleasure. We need to remember this. It is not uncommon that underlying a long pattern of sin is an old, untended wound. When this is the case, we turn to sin not so much for gratification as for numbing.[29] We eat, for example, not because we are hungry, but because we are anxious. We drink, not because we want to be carefree, but to forget our shame. In such circumstances, killing sin requires not only mortifying a passion, but healing a wound. Only if we

---

28. Here is one concrete example. Vanity is endemic in modern America. We put far too much stock in our appearance. In spite of knowing this we build houses that are filled with full-length mirrors. We need to realize that constantly seeing one's own reflection is not normal. Removing such mirrors will not eliminate vanity; however, it may cut off some of the triggers that cause us to focus so much attention on our physical appearance.

29. James Davies writes, 'When we do not confront and solve our primary problems, our secondary problems remain intact. This causes us to become developmentally immobilized or blocked.' See James Davies, *The Importance of Suffering: the Value and Meaning of Emotional Discontent* (New York: Routledge, 2012) p. 89.

uncover the depth of the problem will we be able to treat it and to take away the longstanding provision that sin has been feeding on.[30]

In view of this last point, men need to realize that mortification and Christian counseling will often go hand in hand. One man will be turning to porn simply for the dopamine hit that it provides. Another will use porn as a coping mechanism for loneliness and shame. Neither man is more or less sinful than the other. The actions of both are wrong. Yet the path to recovery will be slightly different for each. The second man will need to go back in order to go forward. He must heal in order to be holy. The first man just needs a stiff rebuke.

Rule 9 – You Need Absolute Trust

'Oh, the depths of the riches and wisdom and knowledge of God! How unsearchable are his judgments and how inscrutable his ways!' (Rom. 11:33).

God's wisdom is higher than ours. There are any number of stories in the Bible in which God used circumstances that were impossible to predict in order to accomplish His purposes. The most stunning examples of this are the incarnation and the crucifixion. No one would have guessed that either was a sign of strength or of victory.

We need to remember the inscrutability of God's purposes as we fight sin. There will be times when we fight resolutely against sin and yet feel no relief or freedom from its oppression. We may even feel as if ground is being relentlessly lost – that the harder we fight, the further back we are driven. Such feelings are not a reason to despair. In any battle there are two perspectives. There is the view from the frontline where men are enmeshed in hand-to-hand combat, and there is the view from the command center where high-ranking

---

30. For more on this topic see Peter Scazzero, *Emotionally Healthy Discipleship: Moving from Shallow Christianity to Deep Transformation* (Grand Rapids: Zondervan, 2021).

officers see the battle as a whole. During the Battle of the Bulge, a lot of GIs, no doubt, felt like the Germans had the upper hand. Tanks had crushed their lines and left them running for cover. Yet, in the end the Nazis lost the battle. More was going on than could be seen from any, single foxhole.[31]

This principle – that our vision is always incomplete – needs to be kept in mind in the war against sin. Anyone familiar with the life of Paul should know that the form of the cross is often repeated in the experience of the believer. It is often those who look like they are losing, or even feel like they are dying, who end up being filled with supernatural strength to complete the mission of God. This should give us comfort in those moments when we are tempted to give up the fight. At such times we should remember the following secret of Paul: 'For when I am weak, then I am strong' (2 Cor. 12:10).

Yet, there is something else we should know about the mysterious way in which dying can lead to life. A marvel of God's wisdom is that He often uses one sin to deal with another.[32] This is especially true of pride. Often, it is only through repeated failure that the walls of pride begin to crack and tumble. It is only when we are humbled by our weakness that we truly look to God for the strength we need.

John Newton captures this truth beautifully in a well-known hymn. This hymn is worth quoting in full:

---

31. John Newton is excellent on this topic. He says, 'A double quantity of real grace, if I may so speak, that has a double quantity of hindrances to conflict with, will not be easily observed, unless these hindrances are likewise known and attended to; and a smaller measure of grace may appear great when its exercise meets with no remarkable obstruction. For these reasons, we can never be competent judges of each other, because we cannot be completely acquainted with the whole complex case.' See John Newton, *Select Letters of John Newton* (Edinburgh: Banner of Truth, 2011).

32. Peter Kreft talks about this in *Back to Virtue: Traditional Moral Wisdom for Modern Moral Confusion* (San Franscisco: Ignatius, 1992), ch. 12. See also John Newton's Letter, 'Advantages from Remaining Sin' in *Select Letters of John Newton*.

SURVIVING THE TRENCHES

I ask'd the Lord that I might grow
In faith, and love, and every grace;
Might more of his salvation know,
And seek more earnestly his face.

'Twas he who taught me thus to pray,
And he, I trust, has answer'd prayer;
But it has been in such a way
As almost drove me to despair.

I hoped that in some favour'd hour
At once he'd answer my request;
And, by his love's constraining power,
Subdue my sins, and give me rest.

Instead of this, he made me feel
The hidden evils of my heart,
And let the angry powers of hell
Assault my soul in every part.

Yea, more, with his own hand he seem'd
Intent to aggravate my woe;
Cross'd all the fair designs I schem'd,
Blasted my gourds, and laid me low.

'Lord, why is this?' I trembling cry'd,
'Wilt thou pursue thy worm to death?'
'Tis in this way,' the Lord reply'd,
'I answer prayer for grace and faith.

'These inward trials I employ
'From self, and pride, to set thee free,
'And break thy schemes of earthly joy,
'That thou may'st seek thy all in me.'[33]

---

33. We often imagine that the ideal road of sanctification would be level and a constant incline. This is not the case. For growth to occur, we need not only to travel up; we also need to go down. Most of the useful knowledge that we learn about ourselves will be in the valley, not on the mountaintop. This is part of God's wisdom.

Rule 10 – Never Give Up

'For sin will have no dominion over you' (Rom. 6:14).

Chesterton wrote an unforgettable ballad about the victory of the English king, Alfred the Great, over the Vikings. The poem opens with an air of darkness and defeat. Alfred and the Saxon army have just had the snot beaten out of them multiple times. The leaders are scattered, the soldiers in disarray, and Alfred himself is having to creep in the shadows to avoid being caught.

One night, while Alfred is musing a final attempt to overthrow the Danes, he has a vision. A lady appears to him and provides a stark assessment of the situation. She says,

> *But you and all the kind of Christ*
> *Are ignorant and brave,*
> *And you have wars you hardly win*
> *And souls you hardly save.*
> *'I tell you naught for your comfort,*
> *Yea, naught for your desire,*
> *Save that the sky grows darker yet*
> *And the sea rises higher.*[34]

No prosperity gospel is set before Alfred. The lady kills any hope that easy victory is on the horizon. She reminds him that one of the mysteries of faith is that God often allows the night to reach pitch black before signaling the sun to rise. Then continuing, she says,

> *Night shall be thrice night over you,*
> *And heaven an iron cope.*[35]
> *Do you have joy without a cause,*
> *Yea, faith without a hope?*

He leads us through trials that disrupt our order, not so that we can live in frustration, but so that we can be reordered. All of this is why no man should be eager to leave 'the valley' until he has learned all that he can from having been cut to his knees.

34. See G. K. Chesterton, *The Ballad of the White Horse* (digital copies available).
35. A 'cope' is something that resembles a long garment or robe.

These last two lines are worth pondering. What does the lady mean by asking whether Alfred has 'joy without a cause?' The meaning is clearer if we restate the question as joy without an *apparent* cause. In truth, Alfred is in the position that every Christian is in all of the time. The joy that must fuel Alfred as he rises for one more battle is the joy that must empower the daily Christian life – a joy that can never be explained by factors that are visible or measurable. Based on the laws of probability, Alfred has no reason to feel anything but dejection. Nothing has changed since his last defeat. And yet, as Christians, former defeat is not a factor in our algebra. The attitude of faith is not built on statistics, but on God.

This takes us to the second line. What is meant by 'faith without hope'? The sense is captured if we substitute 'reasonable expectation' for the word 'hope.' Did Abraham have any reasonable expectation to have a child as an old man? None at all. Yet, he hoped against hope, and the Lord gave him a son. Could Israel reasonably expect that the Red Sea would swallow Pharaoh's army? No. And yet it did. Such is the attitude that the lady is calling Alfred to find – an attitude of free falling self-despair that suddenly finds sure footing in the faithfulness of God.[36]

Tucked away in the middle of Romans 6, Paul makes an astonishing claim. He says, 'For sin will have no dominion over you.' We need to

---

36. Charles Wesley captures this truth magnificently in his hymn 'Father of Jesus Christ, My Lord.'

> *In hope, against all human hope,*
> *Self-desperate, I believe;*
> *Thy quickening word shall raise me up,*
> *Thou shalt Thy Spirit give.*
>
> *Faith, mighty faith, the promise sees,*
> *And looks to that alone;*
> *Laughs at impossibilities,*
> *And cries: It shall be done!*

understand that this remark is not the empty sigh of an optimist. It is not a conditional statement that – in the end – may or may not be true. These are words of promise. Paul is telling us that those who have died with Christ will share in the victory of Christ. God will complete the work that He has begun. This means that, when the dust of history finally settles, we will not be counting points to see whether sin has won against the Spirit or the Spirit against sin. The end result will be a decisive knockout. We will be 'more than conquerors through him who loved us' (Rom. 8:37).

It is this sure victory that lifts our spirits to get off the mat, stand back on our feet, and never give up the fight against sin.

2

The Fight against Deception

◁◁◁♦♦♦▷▷▷

In Genesis we read that Adam was told by God to tend and keep the garden (2:15). Some commentators have read this as a calling not only to cultivate the ground, but to defend it from potential evil. They argue that Adam's response to the serpent should have been militant. Instead of allowing the snake to infiltrate the garden and chit chat with Eve, Adam should have struck it on the head and thrown it over the hedges.

This may or may not be the intended meaning of Genesis. Regardless, it is a useful picture of the role of the executive mind in the human person.[1] God has given human beings the capacity to self-monitor our action. Unlike the animals, there is a part of us that sits in a presidential chair, watching the movements of the heart. Consequently, we can never say that we are coerced into sin. The mind always has the final vote. This is why we are culpable for our choices. After listening to the will and the conscience, the mind has the power of veto: It can either reject or endorse the suggestions of desire.[2]

---

1. For a very interesting model of the executive mind and how it interacts with the human emotion see Jonathan Haidt, *The Happiness Hypothesis: Finding Modern Truth in Old Wisdom* (New York: Basic Books, 2006) and also Haidt's more recent book, *The Righteous Mind: Why Good People Are Divided about Politics and Religion* (New York: Vintage, 2013).

2. Jerry Bridges identifies the danger of thinking of committing sin as defeat rather than disobedience. He says, 'When I say I am defeated by some sin

Once we appreciate the role of the executive mind, we can understand why one of the chief strategies of Satan is to disarm it. Consider for a moment the vulnerability of a building when the alarm system unexpectedly cuts out. With no ability to detect a break-in, thieves can move in and out without any interference. Or think what would happen if the president of the United States suddenly became senile. Who knows what mischief could be caused by malicious staff members pulling levers in the Oval Office? Something very similar to this happens to Christians when their minds are darkened by lies. Sinful passions are able to operate freely. Emotion, rather than understanding, dictates the will. With the watchdog asleep, sin can ravage the heart without the homeowner being aware that anything sinister is going on.[3]

The Path of Deception

Too often, when we think of the deceitfulness of sin, or of the lies of the devil, we recall old cartoons in which the devil sits on one shoulder and an angel on the other. The end result is a boardroom scene in which the benefits and risks of sin are rationally debated. However, this is not how deception occurs. Men do not cheat on their taxes after being convinced by a three-point sermon on the topic. Something

---

I am unconsciously slipping out from under my responsibility. I am saying that something outside of me has defeated me. But when I say I am disobedient that places the responsibility for my sin squarely upon me. We may in fact be defeated, but the reason we are defeated is we have chosen to disobey.' See Jerry Bridges, *Pursuit of Holiness*, p. 80.

3. John Owen notes the particular danger of the mind being deceived in his classic, *Indwelling Sin in Believers*. He says, 'Deceit properly affects the mind; it is the mind that is deceived. When sin attempts any other way of entrance into the soul, as by the affections, the mind, retaining its right and sovereignty, is able to give check and control unto it. But where the mind is tainted, the prevalency must be great .... Hence it is, that though the entanglement of the affections unto sin be oftentimes most troublesome, yet the deceit of the mind is always most dangerous, and that because of the place that it possesseth in the soul as unto its operations. Its office is to guide, direct, choose and lead.' See *Indwelling Sin* (Kindle edition).

more subtle happens. They hear stories of other people cheating and not getting caught; they begin to have a niggling feeling that a little cheating will not hurt anyone, especially Uncle Sam; they convince themselves that the IRS is not watching; they steal a little, then a lot, and so the process continues. The path to sin – at least deep sin – is far more like drifting in a current than being cajoled to jump off of a diving board. By the time the gavel is struck and a decision is made, the conscience is snoring in the balcony.[4]

Yet, how does this drift *begin* to occur? This is a question that needs to be answered. The fight against sin does not begin with the blast of a trumpet and a full-frontal attack by evil desire. The battle begins much earlier as Sin and Satan conspire together to darken the mind. Here propaganda provides a startlingly accurate model for the way in which the devil prepares the heart for sin. Effective propaganda, like effective marketing, makes no attempt to argue. It shows. The aim of effective propaganda is not to convince the mind, but to bypass the mind. The goal is to immerse people in such a dense web of messaging that, over time, what ought to trip an alarm instead feels normal, safe, and true. The role of feeling here needs to be emphasized. A good propagandist knows that once something is felt to be true, it is only a matter of time before it is accepted as true. Likewise, once a message is felt to be true it is only a short time before people begin to conform their behavior to their freshly digested belief.[5]

This is precisely how the process of disarming the mind works. The devil and sin always prefer a cold war to a hot one. Their preferred first

---

4. Jonathan Haidt quotes Robert Wright as saying, 'Human beings are a species splendid in their array of moral equipment, tragic in their propensity to misuse it, and pathetic in their constitutional ignorance of the misuse.' See *The Happiness Hypothesis: Finding Modern Truth in Old Wisdom* (New York: Basic Books, 2006), p. 26.

5. The tactics of propaganda are carefully exposed in Jacques Ellul's *Propaganda: the Formation of Men's Attitudes* (New York: Vintage, 1973).

move is not to carpet bomb the heart with blasts of temptation, but to lull the mind to sleep in a state of delusion. The motive for this is not hard to see: Once the mind is switched off, evil desire can operate without restraint.[6]

A further example will clarify what this looks like in practice. The man who brazenly defiles his marriage vows does not do so after a debate in the pub about the relative merits of adultery. He does not read statistical studies and conclude that men with mistresses are happier than those without. He certainly doesn't read the lives of any Old Testament characters and deduce that polyamory (multiple partners) is a more fulfilling path than monogamy. A more surreptitious process occurs. The man sees the excitement of a secret affair represented on TV; the message 'taboo sex is fun' is repeated through countless pop songs; he listens to friends – even pastors – preach the message, 'God just wants me to be happy.' Sin uses all of this and more to muzzle the conscience. Thus, by the time the man chooses to show up at a motel, he might as well be intoxicated. His grip on reality has been reduced to a pinky finger and a thumb.

Now, in view of this threat, this chapter has two objectives. The first is to diagnose what the mind looks like when it falls asleep. This sleep is evident in four different spiritual attitudes: negligence, indifference, rebellion, and despair. If a man slips into any one of these mental postures, his guard is down. The backdoor is wide open for sinful passions to enter and exit as they please.

The second objective is to show the way in which particular lies feed into these four attitudes. A man does not suddenly wake up

---

6. In Ethel Barrett's retelling of John Bunyan's classic *Holy War*, Diabolus says, 'We'll cajole them, delude them, pretending things that will never be and promising things they shall never get. Lies, lies, lies – the only way to get Mansoul to let us in. And so our intentions will be invisible and we will be invisible.' See *Chronicles of Mansoul* (Glendale: Regal Books, 1969), p. 5.

in a state of moral delusion like he would wake up with a fever or a headache. Delusion is the end result of certain lies being massaged slowly, but steadily, into the heart. This means that the best way to defend the mind is through vigilant lie detecting. The more adept we are at spotting and exposing the propaganda of sin, the more protected we will be from lapsing into the defenseless postures of negligence, indifference, rebellion, or despair.[7]

Negligence and the Lies That Feed It

The fall of Troy is a cautionary tale. After long years of warfare, the Trojans looked out from their walls one morning and were surprised to see the camp of the Greek warriors deserted. Carefully, the Trojans opened the gates of their city and searched the outer lands for signs of what had happened. Eventually, they made their way to the beaches. All of the Greek ships were gone. The only thing present was a large wooden structure in the shape of a horse. After debating what to do, finally, the Trojans decided to bring the horse into their city. This mistake led to the end of a once great civilization. Little did the Trojans know that Greek soldiers were hidden within the horse and that the Greek ships were tucked out of sight in a nearby bay. That night, while the citizens of Troy were adjusting to a new life of peace, Greek soldiers snuck out of the horse and opened the gates of the city. The rest is embers and ashes.

This famous story is an emblem of the spiritual danger of negligence. One of the chief schemes of sin is to lure us away from our defenses so

---

7. Modern men would be more vigilant if they heeded the warning of John Calvin: 'Being forewarned of the constant presence of an enemy the most daring, the most powerful, the most crafty, the most indefatigable, the most completely equipped with all the engines, and the most expert in the science of war, let us not allow ourselves to be overtaken by sloth or cowardice, but, on the contrary, with minds aroused and ever on the alert, let us stand ready to resist; and, knowing that this warfare is terminated only by death, let us study to persevere.' See John Calvin, *Institutes of the Christian Religion* trans. Henry Beveridge (Grand Rapids: Eerdmans, 1997), 1.14.

that we are vulnerable, relaxed, and unprotected. Sin wants to do to us what the Greeks did to the Trojans: to catch us off guard so that it can conquer and subdue us.

The key to countering this strategy is detecting the lies that lead to a negligent state of mind. Each of these lies is like a Trojan horse. If we reject it early on the beach it cannot harm us. However, if we entertain it in our hearts, we will soon discover that the walls of self-control are of no use because the enemy has found a way to open the gates from the inside.[8]

Lie 1 – 'I can linger at the doorstep of sin.'

Willpower is weak. No man should rely upon it except as a last resort. In most cases, people who appear to have an inflexible will in fact have something altogether different. They have wisdom. Avoiding temptation is always easier than resisting temptation.[9]

Any man who finds himself loitering at the door of sin needs to remember the story of Alypius, Augustine's youthful companion. Alypius was known and regarded for his purity. Unlike most other young men in Rome at the time, he refused to go and watch the gladiator fights in the Colosseum. Yet, one day a group of friends badgered Alypius into stepping into the magnificent arena. Alypius consented with one condition: He said that he would sit in the arena, but he would not open his eyes. He lived up to his word – for a while, but then something happened. Tens of thousands of spectators erupted with cheers. As quickly as Alypius' eyes slipped open, something else slipped in. A lust for bloodshed rushed into his heart.

---

8. A much more extensive list of lies can be found in Thomas Brooks' classic work, *Precious Remedies against Satan's Devices*. Two classic allegories that chart the role of delusion in entrenching sin are John Bunyan's *Holy War* and John Amos Comenius' *Labyrinth of the World and Paradise of the Heart*. Both allegories are outstanding manuals for learning the art of spiritual warfare.

9. James Clear makes this point more than once in *Atomic Habits: An Easy Way to Build Good Habits and Break Bad Ones* (New York: Avery, 2018).

Before he knew what was going on, he was high fiving friends and cheering on his feet.[10]

Sadly, this moment was a turning point in Alypius' life. From then on, he switched from being known for his purity to being known as a passionate recruiter, pulling in other friends to go and see the Roman games.

It is worth asking the question, where did Alypius go wrong? The answer is not the moment when he opened his eyes. That was a near inevitable consequence of a prior choice. He went wrong when he consented to going into the Colosseum. At that point the game was rigged. It was only a matter of time before willpower would snap under the pressure of temptation.

Proverbs 5:8 is clear. The best way to resist sin is by avoiding the door of temptation. Only an attitude of negligence would make us think that we could window-shop without eventually making a purchase.

Lie 2 – 'I can manage my sin.'

During the Cold War, the US government's policy toward communism was one of containment. The United States had no strategy for eliminating communism; the goal, rather, was to restrict its spread. Many Christians have a similar policy toward sin. Rather than take up the New Testament call to 'put to death the deeds of the body' (Rom. 8:13), they are happy to cohabit with sin so long as its growth is limited. The problem is that sin is a power that refuses to be contained. To attempt to make peace with a known sin is like negotiating with a terrorist group. The only peace terrorists are interested in is the peace of fear, subjection, and conquest. So it is with sin.

A classic case study of such naivety is seen in the life of David. David thought that he could manage the sinful passion of lust. He could have an affair with a neighbor's wife while controlling the

---

10. See book six of Augustine's *Confessions* for the story of Alypius.

collateral damage. He quickly learned otherwise. Before David could catch his breath, adultery was producing deceit, which was producing murder, which was producing a callous and indifferent pride. One sin led to another with the spontaneity and speed of a falling train of dominoes. Although, in the end, David's sin was fully forgiven, the consequences were not mopped up without residue. Bitter side effects of a single choice continued to plague David for years to come.

Men need to ponder the warning of David's fall. Sin is not something to be managed; it is something to be killed. This is a truth that we neglect to our peril. And the sooner we kill sin, the better, because the longer we wait, the more difficult the process will be to pick up the pieces of the life we have shattered.

Lie 3 – 'There is no hook in the bait.'

In the US it is not uncommon to see a commercial on TV for some new drug that promises to heal a frustrating disease such as psoriasis or rheumatoid arthritis. After mentioning the positive benefits and likelihood of success, the advertisement goes on to list all of the risks and potential side effects associated with the treatment. Typically, this list of potential cancers and major organ malfunctions is narrated while the camera drifts to children laughing on swings and a dad playing fetch with a golden retriever. What is the logic of the marketing? Drug manufacturers want their audience to focus on the good, the bait, while ignoring the danger, the hook.

Satan attempts to do something similar with sin.[11] He advertises the pleasure and momentary relief of sin, but hides the fact that the wages of sin are always death. To outsmart the devil, Christians need to identify the hook in temptation. They need to understand that there

---

11. The elder demon in *The Screwtape Letters* says, 'It is funny how mortals always picture us as putting things into their minds: in reality our best work is done by keeping things out.' See C. S. Lewis, *The Screwtape Letters*, p. 22.

is more hope of getting enjoyment out of a poisonous mushroom than getting any lasting comfort from sin. The river of pleasure ebbs from the feet of the Most High. To look for satisfaction anywhere other than God – especially in a direction that is opposed to God – is as useless as traveling to a desert in search of water. Only a negligent heart would forget this truth.

Indifference and the Lies That Feed It

Every pastor has had the following experience. John is an upstanding member of the congregation. Late one Tuesday night, you get a call from someone in the church that John has just left his wife and run off with a colleague from work. Dumbfounded, you call a couple of elders, make contact with John, and organize a meeting to address the problem. The meeting occurs. You lay out the case. You point to the unquestionable Bible references about marriage, fidelity, and commitment. You remind John of his church membership vows. After hearing all of this, what does John do? Like a teenager ignoring a parent, he shrugs his shoulders, declares that he's never felt so alive, and joyfully skips down the path of iniquity with the enthusiasm of a child playing hopscotch.

What is going on when this happens? A bizarre numbing of mind has occurred, a moral indifference to the reality and consequences of sin. Ideally, the mind would be like a prosecuting attorney working alongside the conscience to convict a man of trespasses. Yet, the mind often falls short of this calling. Having swallowed and digested a variety of lies, the mind shifts sides. Instead of prosecuting sin, the mind joins the defense.[12] Suddenly, the faculty that God has given us in order to pursue the light is used to pursue the darkness. This is a harrowing state of affairs, one that begins with indifference, but if

---

12. On this point Benjamin Franklin is famous for saying, 'So convenient a thing is it to be a reasonable creature, since it enables one to find or make a reason for everything one has a mind to do.'

not stopped in due time, will eventually lead to harder dispositions of rebellion and even hatred.

How do we avoid this slippery slope of indifference? A good start is to familiarize ourselves with the following lies.

Lie 1 – 'I could do worse.'

Men often try to dilute the evil of sin by comparing what has been done with what could have been done. Pornography does not feel like a flagrant foul if juxtaposed against a more public sin like adultery. Set beside physical violence, verbal abuse is trifling. Slothfulness and gluttony at home are much slighter offenses than getting drunk at a bar or experimenting with illegal substances – at least so we tell ourselves. This logic needs to be exposed for what it is, *ridiculous*. The measure of a sin is never how far it is from the basement of Hell, but how far it is from the ceiling of heaven. God did not say, 'Be better than thy neighbor.' He said, 'Be holy for I am holy' (cf. Lev. 19:2, 1 Pet. 1:16).

Here is a question worth pondering: Why did Israel struggle incessantly, repeatedly, and uniformly with idolatry? The answer is because idolatry felt normal. Never in the history of the world, until Sinai, had anyone said that making idols was wrong. Every culture adjacent to Israel made use of idols. Carved images were as ubiquitous in the Ancient Near East as smart phones are in America. Therefore, since idol worship did not *feel* evil, a lot of Israelites made the mistake of thinking that idol worship *was* not evil. They confused feeling for truth.

This confusion was not accidental. It was part of a sinister plan hatched by Satan, a strategy he is still employing today. Satan loves nothing more than to dilute the shame of sin, to numb its discomfort, and to erase its boundaries so that God's own people begin to accuse *Him* of being legalistic. Kierkegaard says, 'Most people believe that the Christian commandments are intentionally a little too severe – like putting the clock on half an hour to make sure of not being late in the morning.'[13] But God's wisdom is not high-strung. It is exact and purposeful. To doubt the judgment of the Almighty is to play into the hand of a diabolical strategy. Satan would like nothing more than for men to think they are doing God a favor by choosing a minor offense rather than a major one. This would be a double-win for Satan. Not only would a sinful action itself be chosen, but an undetected attitude of indifference would darken the mind. Men would take one step forward along the path of not caring about their sin.

Lie 2 – 'This makes me happy.'

Let's go back to the story of John who left his wife for a co-worker. In such circumstances, which are not at all uncommon, what is the lie that makes men willing to crush their wives and emotionally batter their children? Often, it is the belief that personal happiness trumps personal holiness. Men trample the purity and sacredness of marriage for no better reason than that they miss the feeling of being a teenager in high school.

It's hard to think of any lie embedded more deeply in pop culture than the idea that fun and happiness are the ultimate court of appeals. A key facet of modern identity is the belief that self-fulfillment and self-indulgence are one and the same thing, that the only trustworthy guide to lasting joy is the voice of untamed desire.[14]

Sadly, a lot of Christians have swallowed and digested this lie. They sincerely believe that the purchase of happiness is worth the price of sin. It's not. Jesus once told a story about an anonymous rich man and a poor man named Lazarus. The rich man had the Walt Disney version of life. Every day was a sumptuous feast. Meanwhile, Lazarus spent his

---

13. Soren Kierkegaard, *Papers and Journals: A Selection* (New York: Penguin, 1996).
14. Carl Trueman traces the development of these modern assumptions by reviewing nineteenth-century Romanticism and twentieth-century Freudian psychology. See Carl Trueman, *The Rise and Triumph of the Modern Self: Cultural Amnesia, Expressive Individualism, and the Road to Sexual Revolution* (Wheaton: Crossway, 2020).

days dumpster diving. Both men eventually died, and then the tables turned. Whereas the poor man found a seat at Abraham's bosom, the rich man landed in the smoking landfill of Hell.

It does not take a PI to crack the meaning of the story: The road to Hell is not just paved with good intentions; it is also paved with quick and easy pleasure. There is nothing wrong with celebrating life or enjoying the gift of happiness. Yet, no measure of happiness is worth the price of the smallest of sins.[15]

Lie 3 – 'All men struggle with X.'

Many of us have experienced accountability gone wrong. A group of men meet regularly to talk about their struggle with pornography. The first guy raises his hand and admits to failing this week. The second guy does the same. As the circle gets completed the batting average is identical. There is not a single testimony of success. When this happens, something disturbing often occurs. Rather than men repenting of their sin, their sin is subtly affirmed. If everyone is struggling with lust, the thought surfaces that maybe lust isn't that bad after all. Guys walk away from the meeting feeling much better about themselves, but entirely for the wrong reason. No authentic transaction with the cross has occurred. Sin has not been rejected; it has been normalized.

---

15. Thomas Watson gives a terrifying picture of the hopelessness of Hell. He says, 'Oh eternity! If all the body of earth and sea were turned to sand, and all the air up to the starry heaven were nothing but sand, and a little bird should come every thousand years, and fetch away in her bill but the tenth part of a grain of all that heap of sand, what numberless years would be spent before that vast heap of sand would be fetched away! Yet, if at the end of all that time, the sinner might come out of hell, there would be some hope; but that word "Ever" breaks the heart. "The smoke of their torment ascendeth up for ever and ever." What a terror is this to the wicked, enough to put them into a cold sweat, to think, as long as God is eternal, He lives forever to be avenged upon them!' *Could any sin be worth this?* See Thomas Watson, *The Body of Divinity*, pp. 62-63.

Men need the X-ray vision to see straight through this pattern of deception. Joining a crowd to lynch a man is no better than committing an act of individual murder. There is no safety in numbers when it comes to sin. There is no place to hide.[16] The Bible is clear that each of us will face a personal judgment. Paul says in 2 Corinthians 5:10, 'For we must all appear before the judgment seat of Christ, so that each one may receive what is due for what he has done in the body, whether good or evil.' To resist sin, we must always have this judgment in view.[17]

Likewise, to combat the normalization of sin, men must keep in mind that our model of righteousness is not our peer-group, but the person of Jesus. Although we may never attain to His absolute purity, we can never be content with anything less. It is, after all, to His image that we are being conformed (cf. Rom. 8:29). Jesus is the standard of holiness in heaven; He is also the standard of holiness on earth. We cannot permit an attitude of indifference to blind us from this truth.[18]

Lie 4 – 'It's not my fault.'

We live in a broken world. Inevitably, this means that every heart is wounded; every set of parents is inadequate; no society is truly just. We not only contribute sins to the stockpile of the world, but also inherit the toxic conditions of the moral evil committed by

---

16. The prophet Amos gives a horrifying picture of the impossibility of escaping divine judgment. God says through the prophet, 'If they dig into Sheol, from there shall my hand take them; if they climb up to heaven, from there I will bring them down. If they hide themselves on the top of Carmel, from there I will search them out and take them; and if they hide from my sight at the bottom of the sea, there I will command the serpent, and it shall bite them. And if they go into captivity before their enemies, there I will command the sword, and it shall kill them; and I will fix my eyes upon them for evil and not for good' (Amos 9:2-4).

17. John Calvin affirms this need by stating that the godly man 'keeps the judgment-seat always in view.' See John Calvin, *Institutes of the Christian Religion*, 1.2.

18. No one has exposed the clever ways in which we avoid the standards of holiness more compellingly than William Law in *A Serious Call to a Devout and Holy Life*.

others.[19] All of this needs to be recognized. All of this needs to be factored in as people seek healing by the grace of God. However, there is one line that a Christian can never cross. I can never say of my sin, 'It was not my fault.'

God is clear on this point: each individual is accountable for his sin.[20] This means, for example, that even while we might see a connection between the pain of trauma and sinful behavior, we cannot blame the behavior on the trauma. To do this would be to take a fatalistic view of sin. It would cancel personal responsibility in such a way as to say that circumstances, not the self, are the guilty party.

In practice, this means that our history cannot make us feel indifferent toward our sin. We cannot feel as if we get a free pass from struggling against sinful desire because there was abuse in our background or because our parents were callous and detached. Instead, we need to do something far different. We need to recognize that where there is deep pain, there is need for deep healing. We must look to Christ to make us whole even as we look to Him to make us holy.[21]

---

19. Gabor Mate comments, 'As a rule, whatever we don't deal with in our lives, we pass on to our children. Our unfinished emotional business becomes theirs ... Children swim in their parents' unconscious like fish swim in the sea.' See *In the Realm of Hungry Ghosts: Close Encounters with Addiction* (Berkeley: North Atlantic Books, 2010), p. 253.

20. David Powlison tactfully makes this point in *Safe and Sound: Standing Firm in Spiritual Battles* (Greensboro: New Growth Press, 2019). Although we are not responsible *in any way* for the sins that other people commit against us, we are responsible for our own actions. Now determining what is sin and what is not sin is a difficult question that often requires pastoral care to resolve. We cannot always trust the emotions of guilt and shame. We must listen to the wisdom of others to help us discern the difference between legitimate sin and imaginary guilt.

21. For thinking about the need for wholeness, consider the following lines from one of Charles Wesley's hymns:

> *Deepen the wound Thy hands have made*
> *In this weak, helpless soul;*
> *Till mercy, with its kindly aid,*
> *Descends to make me whole.*

Rebellion and the Lies That Feed It

In the seventeenth-century there was brutal persecution of Christians in Japan. Christians would be rounded up and brought to the center of a village or city. Officials would then place a fumie on the ground, which was an image of Jesus' face, and give a strict order to trample on it. Thus, believers were left with a dreadful choice: either submit to the order by rejecting Christ or else refuse and suffer painful torture, often leading to death.[22]

At one level we can rightly say that all sin is rebellion. Yet, we can also say that not all sin is rebellious in the same way. Men who are negligent, or indifferent, do indeed willfully transgress the laws of God. Yet, there is often a bumbling aspect to their gait. They are staggering in a manner that demonstrates that they are only half-conscious of what they are doing.

If possible, sin desires to drive men into a state of moral delusion that is even darker and more sinister than this. We might label this state *rebellion proper*. In this condition men are fully aware of what they are doing. They see a path of sin; they see a path of righteousness; and then they chart their course deliberately and decisively away from the Lord. When this happens, men might as well be stepping on the face of Jesus (cf. Heb. 10:26-31). The problem is not that we lose sight of Him for a moment, but rather we take Him for granted. We are willing to use Him for our own wicked purposes.

What would bring a man – a professing Christian man – to this dark place? Once again, lies are the seedbed of the attitude. First,

---

> *The sharpness of Thy two-edged sword*
> *Enable me to endure;*
> *Till bold to say: My hallowing Lord*
> *Hath wrought a perfect cure.*

22. On this horrific era of persecution see Shusako Endo's unforgettable novel *Silence* trans. William Johnston (New York: Picador, 2016).

we passively allow deceit to be sown in the heart; next, the roots of delusion set in.

For any men who are horrified by the thought of deliberate, premeditated sin, the following lies deserve special notice.

Lie 1 – 'God is all love and no justice.'

At St. Catherine's Monastery in Egypt there is an icon of Jesus. At first glance His face looks disfigured. There is no symmetry in His facial expression. However, after looking at the image for a minute, its design becomes clear. If one side of the face is covered, Jesus' face is severe, the countenance of an angry lord who has come to punish wicked servants. If the other side of the face is covered, the opposite expression appears. All that is evident is the lamb-like visage of a gentle and gracious brother.

It's a sad fact that a lot of preaching has covered one half of the face of God. The only message that some men have heard is a message of a loving God who cannot bear to see a child in pain. No one has had the courage to tell them soberly what a fearful thing it is to fall into the hands of the living God (Heb. 10:31). This distortion of truth has left a lot of men in a perilous position. Deep down they don't think that sin is really that big of a deal. They don't think that the nature of God is such that He would really judge a sinner. Their understanding of God is more along the lines of a doting grandmother than a consuming fire. They sin boldly thinking that, no matter what choices they make, God will always be there to tuck them in at night.[23]

---

23. Richard Loveless helpfully shows the way in which God's love and wrath must be understood in relation to one another. He says, 'It is only in the light of the revelation through the cross of God's overwhelming love for his creation that we can understand his anger against the distortion or destruction of that creation. The cross, in fact, is the perfect statement both of God's wrath against sin and of the depth of his love and mercy in the recovery of the damaged creation and its damagers. God's mercy, patience, and love must be fully preached in the church.

We need to expose the lie behind this attitude. Is God merciful? Immeasurably so. However, the mercy of God does not negate the justice of God. Men who are using the kindness of God as an excuse for sin need to contemplate Galatians 6:7-8: 'Do not be deceived: God is not mocked, for whatever one sows, that will he also reap. For the one who sows to his own flesh will from the flesh reap corruption, but the one who sows to the Spirit will from the Spirit reap eternal life.'

Lie 2 – 'Repentance is easy.'

Anyone who believes that repentance is easy has never actually repented. The heart is made of a quick-drying cement that hardens in an instant but takes hours, days – sometimes years – to break. Recognizing this, no one is more foolish than the person who goes into a sin thinking that he can quickly find his way back out again. There is an old Greek story about a wicked king, Minos of Crete, who built a labyrinth so intricate that no one could escape from it. To make matters worse, Minos put a man-eating Minotaur in the midst of the labyrinth that was always hungry – and searching – for food. This story provides a sobering picture of the reality of sin. Getting into a sinful pattern of behavior is as easy as making a credit card transaction. Getting out of a sinful pattern of behavior is as difficult as escaping from a cruel and bewildering maze.

In view of this, Christians should take care whenever they hear the voice of Satan whispering, 'You can always repent afterwards.' We must remember that Satan's objective is not to maim, but to kill. He wants to lure us into a maze that will confuse, disorient, depress, and if possible, incapacitate us. Knowing this, we should no more play with

---

But they are not credible unless they are presented in tension with God's infinite power, complete and sovereign control of the universe, holiness and righteousness.' See Richard Loveless, *Dynamics of Spiritual Life: An Evangelical Renewal of Theology* (Wheaton: IVP, 2020), p. 84.

temptation than we would play with a pit-viper. Repentance may be free, but it is not easy.

Lie 3 – 'Sin is already paid for.'

I wish I could say that a Christian man will never succumb to this mindset, that he will never be so perverted as to use the once-for-all sacrifice of Christ as an excuse to commit a sin. But the fact is that most of us have entertained this thought, even acted upon it. We have brazenly walked straight up to the bar of temptation, ordered a sin, and told the host to put the guilt on the tab of Jesus.

How does a man reach this despicable frame of mind? The answer is by thinking that grace is a right rather than a gift, that salvation is a mechanism rather than a miracle. Sin wants us to lose sight of the fact that a living and breathing man named Jesus actually had nails driven through His hands in order to pay the penalty of our sin.[24] Instead, sin proposes that we think of our justification as a math equation: sin + sacrifice = atonement. Though the formula is mathematically correct, it is as impersonal as a lab report. Reduced to such terms, Calvary feels more like a money transfer than a rescue by blood.

Men who are on the brink of thinking that they can pull grace from heaven like they can pour water from the tap need to answer the following questions. Would you desecrate and burn the flag of your country? Would you pour your sewage on the graves of your parents? If not – if you hold these lesser goods as objects of untouchable honor – how, then, can you willfully trample on the body of Jesus? Only an attitude of rebellion could inspire such callous indifference.[25]

---

24. To be reminded of the suffering of Christ men should read Isaac Watts' hymn 'Infinite Grief! Amazing Woe!'
25. In truth, no man in this condition should have any assurance of his salvation. Thomas Watson says, 'Sanctification is the seed; assurance is the flower that grows out of it.' Men who have questions about assurance should read Watson's full treatment of the topic in *A Body of Divinity*. Digital copies are available online.

Lie 4 – 'No one can see.'

In Proverbs we read that, 'The fool says in his heart there is no God.' As any pastor will point out, the text is not speaking to theoretical atheists. We know this because there were no such atheists in the Ancient Near East. The text, rather, is referring to practical atheists, people who choose to sin because they think that no one is looking.

The foolishness of this mindset is evident to anyone who knows anything about the Living God. On this point, God speaks through Jeremiah:

> 'Am I a God near at hand,' says the LORD, 'And not a God afar off? Can anyone hide himself in secret places, So that I shall not see him?' says the LORD; 'Do I not fill heaven and earth?' says the LORD (23:23 NKJV).

The answer to these questions is meant to be obvious. No one can hide anything from the blazing eyes of the Living God. From the cupboards of Hell to the windows of heaven, from the tiniest quark to the vastest constellation, from the most bustling crowd to the faintest intuition, God is present everywhere and sees and hears everything. This ought to be a sober warning to men who have convinced themselves that their hypocrisy has gone undetected. They need to reflect on the following truth: 'No creature is hidden from his sight, but all are naked and exposed to the eyes of him to whom we must give account' (Heb. 4:13).

Despair and the Lies That Feed It

Satan's tool belt of lies is diverse. At times he tries to lure us into sin by waxing a shine on forbidden fruit. Other times he tries to keep us in sin by making us believe that God's arm is too short to save and His ear too heavy to hear. He doesn't care about how he snares us. The only thing that matters to him is that we end up tightly bound in a web of deception.

All of us have experienced the feedback loop of sin and despair. First you sin. Then you feel ashamed for what you have done. Next despair sets in – the sense that nothing can be done to fix the problem. Then you sin again because, oddly enough, the thing that brought you grief now offers *temporary* relief from the pain. Though the cycle is irrational, it is effective. It is a whirlpool that is hard to escape once a man is caught in its current.

In *Pilgrim's Progress* we see a terrifying image of what can happen if despair is permitted to settle into a fixed state of mind. At the House of the Interpreter, Christian, the main character of the story, is shown a man who sits like a trapped animal in a cage. No authority has committed him to this prison. He has not been locked in from the outside. Rather it is his own despair that has entrapped the man. The habit of navel-gazing at his own sin has cut off his ability to look up and see a Savior.

Here we see the scary truth that a mindset of despair can be every bit as dangerous as rebellion or indifference. Therefore, men need to be on guard to catch early symptoms of hopelessness before the disease has time to infiltrate the heart. These common lies are particularly lethal.

Lie 1 – 'I am too far gone.'

It is not accidental that the stories of Judas and Peter are interwoven during the trial of Jesus. In reading the stories, it is hard to calculate which of these men committed the more grievous crime. Judas handed Christ over to the authorities; however, Peter, with oaths and swearing, denied Christ three times. In the contest of 'Whose Sin Is Uglier?' the scales are pretty well balanced. Both men were guilty of capital offenses.

Yet, what is most startling as we set these men beside each other is not where each man begins, but where he ends. Peter found mercy and was restored as a friend of Jesus. Judas wrapped a noose of shame around his neck and broke his body on the rocks of despair.

Sin would like nothing more than for us to swallow the lie of Judas, to think that we are too far down the path of iniquity to about-face and come home. All Christians need to resist this lie like we should resist a capsule of cyanide. Before despair conceives in the mind, we need to ask the following questions: When did Jesus ever turn away a broken heart? What leper did He refuse to heal because of his defilement? Is there a single instance in the Bible of someone asking for grace and being rejected? These questions should lead us to one incontestable conclusion: If there was mercy for a dying thief on the cross, if there was forgiveness for an adulterous disciple like Peter, if a scoundrel like Paul could be lifted to the office of an apostle, then there is hope for *me*. I, too, can be forgiven if I relinquish my pride – *and my despair* – and run to the feet of Jesus.

Lie 2 – 'God is more just than merciful.'

We need to recall the image of Jesus as painted at Saint Catherine's monastery. If covering the severe aspect of Jesus' face results in a misinterpretation of His character, so does covering the merciful side. If there is a danger of whitewashing the justice of God, there is an equal danger of plastering over His love. In truth, the image of God as having two opposing profiles is a theological mistake. God is not part justice and part love. His character is 100 per cent both. He is wholly just and wholly loving. This is why there is no tug-of-war going on in the heart of God. All of His love is just, and all of His justice is loving.[26]

If we want to see this profound truth worked out in action the supreme example is the cross. At Calvary we see a justice that crushes sin while simultaneously seeing a love that forgives sinners. Here one part of God's character is not set against another part. Rather, through

---

26. John Stott helpfully remarks, 'The cross of Christ is the event in which God makes known His holiness and His love simultaneously in one event in an absolute manner.' He goes on to show further how it is only in the cross that we learn that 'His holiness and His love are equally infinite.' See John Stott, *The Cross of Christ* (Downers Grove: IVP, 2006), p. 131.

the prism of the cross, the light of holiness is refracted such that perfect justice and perfect mercy are seen to flow from a single heart.

Practically, this means that the cross is always an invitation for sinners to come and receive forgiveness from God. Only at the cross is the awfulness of divine justice revealed in such a way that beckons the sinner to come closer to God rather than to flee in terror. The reason for this is that, in Jesus, God Himself is seen bearing the weight of sin. Without diluting the evil of sin by a drop, Calvary reveals a love that is willing to bear all in order that slaves of darkness can be adopted as children of light.

Sin will labor ceaselessly to twist our understanding of God. In one season of life, we will focus exclusively on His love and mercy; at another, we will concentrate solely on His justice and wrath. How do we avoid teetering from one position to the other? The only answer is to pitch our tent at Calvary. The cross alone provides the stable ground we need in order to avoid stumbling down the verge of rebellion or toppling over the ridge of despair.

Lie 3 – 'My sin is my savior.'

Part of the psychology of addiction is that an addict cannot imagine a different existence for himself. The problem is not simply one of despair; it is one of dependency. The insightful writer Gabor Mate defines addiction as follows: *'any repeated behavior, substance related or not, in which a person feels compelled to persist, regardless of its negative impact on his life and the lives of others.'* [27] The word compelled is of particular interest here. Addictive behavior is driven by a sense of need. The addict sincerely believes that he cannot cope without a particular substance or behavior.

The above paragraph could be rewritten substituting the word sin for addiction. Both are subject to the same lie. Sin desires to drive us

---

27. Gabor Mate, *In the Realm of Hungry Ghosts*, p. 224.

into a posture of submission and dependency. It wants us to believe that if we stopped a specific behavior, then we would no longer be able to endure life.

This, of course, is deception of the worst kind. Living water is not found in porn, or drunkenness, or binge eating, or self-harm. It is found in Jesus, the fountain of eternal life. Threatened by the fear that we will die of thirst without our secret sin, we need to hear afresh the invitation of Christ: 'If anyone thirsts, let him come to me and drink. He who believes in me, as the Scripture has said, out of his heart will flow rivers of living water' (John 7:37-38).[28] It is only Christ that can bring deep and enduring satisfaction to our souls. Any voice that suggests otherwise needs to be identified as a puppet of Satan and resisted with the vigilance that Odysseus resisted the Sirens on his journey back to Ithaca.

The Path to Watchfulness

We need to end this chapter with a difficult question: How will a man develop a watchful mind given the deceitfulness of his heart, the propaganda of the world, and the lies of the devil? There is no quick and simple solution to the predicament. If watchfulness were easy to maintain, governments would not have to spend billions of dollars shifting soldiers from location to location, trying to maintain a spirit of combat-readiness. Yet, despite the challenge, like any other habit, the mind can be trained to grow in vigilance. This, indeed, is part of what it means to present our members as weapons of righteousness to God (cf. Rom. 6:13). Using the Scriptures as a

---

28. An additional lie that could be treated here is the fear that a person has committed an unforgivable sin. This is a particularly difficult lie to extract from some sensitive hearts. Anyone who struggles with such anxiety would benefit from reading John Bunyan's autobiography, *Grace Abounding* and reflecting on the hymns of William Cowper.

whetstone, the bluntest of minds can be made more alert. Bit by bit we can develop the mental dispositions needed to fulfill the following words of Christ: 'Watch and pray that you may not enter into temptation' (Matt. 26:41).

Practically, here are five pieces of advice for men who feel themselves drifting toward the dangerous crags of negligence, indifference, rebellion, and despair. This advice focuses on key practices that will padlock the backdoor of the mind in order to keep lies from slipping in unnoticed. These practices are not quick fixes. They will not produce change overnight. But if taken seriously they will slowly fix the posture of the mind so that, instead of slouching, a man is positioned eyes-up, shoulders back, fists tight – ready for an attack.

1 – Develop the Habit of Practicing the Presence of God

The Roman philosopher Seneca used to tell his disciples that, in order to avoid vice, they ought to imagine themselves always to be in the company of three or four illustrious Romans. We can one-up this as Christians by cultivating the consciousness of living in the presence – not of holy men – but of a holy God. Most of us would behave differently if there was a cable television station dedicated to broadcasting our lives to the public, 24/7. The truth is even more unnerving than this. We live before a God who not only sees the outside, but the inside – the heart, mind, motivation, imagination, and will. The more attentive we are to the presence of God, the less powerful temptation will be. Satan loves nothing more than to convince Christians that the cameras of heaven are off and that no one is watching. We need to bust this myth. Nothing will more effectively promote vigilance than an ongoing awareness that the eyes of heaven are upon us. This spiritual self-consciousness will counteract negligence and indifference regarding sin. It will also buffer us from a rebellious attitude that would think that holiness can be trampled upon free of consequences.

2 – Don't Neglect the Means of Grace

King Saul made many mistakes during his reign. One of the worst was a rash vow in the midst of a heated battle that none of his soldiers could eat until evening. The effect of this vow was to cut men off from the very nourishment that they needed to persist in the fight. Sadly, a lot of Christian men repeat Saul's error. They neglect the very resources that God uses to strengthen and fortify the faith and obedience of Christians. How many men are relaxed about skipping church, reading the Bible, or fellowshipping closely with other men? This behavior is every bit as foolish as fasting before a marathon. If men want to be strong when faced with severe temptation, they need to take every advantage given to be nourished in faith, hope, and love. In practice, this means the following: don't miss church, don't *not* read the Bible, don't *not* pray. Always view negligence as a first step toward sin. Always believe that the surest way to get caught in the net of the flatterer is to ignore the God-ordained channels of truth.

3 – Resist Forcefully the First Movements of Sin

Pompey the Great was one of the greatest military leaders of the ancient world. And yet he ended up being defeated by Julius Caesar and having his head cut off by the Egyptians. How did this happen? The catalyst of Pompey's downfall occurred when rumors began to reach Rome that Caesar was moving with an army toward the city, and Pompey casually did nothing. In fact, Pompey famously said, 'If Pompey the Great stamps his feet, the people will run to assist him.' In fact, they did not. Pompey learned the hard way that early carelessness leads to final defeat.

Too many Christian men repeat this blunder. Rather than resist the first movement of sin, they are passive about detecting lies and killing evil desires. They allow the seed of sin to fall on their hearts and do nothing to remove it before it takes root. Such men need to remember the example of Pompey. It is much better to strike quickly and eliminate the problem than to sit back and wait for the enemy to gain strength.[29]

4 – Confess Any Enjoyment of Sin to a Christian Friend

The favored tactic of sin is to bypass thought and delay choice until the deep desires of the heart are taken captive. Curiosity, interest, desire, fantasy, delight – these are the tentacles of sin that silently stretch forth to strangle a Christian (cf. James 1:15). Long before a man consents to having an affair, or rationalizes cheating on his wife, he first permits himself to linger in the space of temptation. He seeks out the company of a co-worker. He goes out of his way to schedule lunch appointments. He replays the fun of hanging out in spare moments of the day. Curiosity and enjoyment are the gateway drugs to bigger and more destructive actions.

Men need to nip the bud of temptation by confessing to a brother the fact that a dangerous delight has been conceived. The effects of this transparency will be twofold. On the one hand, accountability will reinforce willpower. The encouragement – even rebuke – of a friend will offer resistance to the lure of sin. On the other hand, the friend will not be influenced by what psychologists call 'confirmation bias.' He will see straight through self-deception and rationalization and – assuming he is a resolute Christian – will expose lies already lodged in the heart.[30]

---

29. Thomas Chalmers says, 'The same gospel which sheds an oblivion over all the sinfulness of your past lives, enters upon a war of extermination against all your future sinfulness. You have not yet come under its economy at all, if you have not embarked on the struggle of all your powers and all your purposes with the power of iniquity over you – nor would we say of you, on the one hand, that grace has abounded unto the forgiveness of sin, unless we saw of you, on the other, an honest and determined habit of exertion against the continuance of sin.' See Thomas Chalmers, *Lectures on Romans Vol. 2*, p. 55.

30. Men need to remember S. L. A. Marshall's advice to men preparing for combat: 'When you prepare to fight, you must prepare to talk. You must learn

5 – Begin Each Day Praying through 'St. Patrick's Breastplate'

If we do not believe that we are in danger, we will see no need to be vigilant. One of the great delusions of Western culture is the myth that the world is a playground, and the chief object of life is having fun. This is a disturbing lie. I've never seen a child put on armor to go onto a jungle gym. There is good reason for this: No protection is required to climb up and down a slide. Men need to keep watch lest they succumb to such a carefree attitude. One way of doing so is by reminding ourselves daily that we are stepping out onto a battlefield. The more aware we are of the threats around us, the more alert we will be in general. Vigilance will set in as a habit of mind.[31]

One outstanding way of inculcating this mindset is to begin each morning by reciting St. Patrick's Breastplate. This classic prayer, used for centuries, will do two things: First, it will remind men of their need for protection in order to fight sin; second, it will remind men that the only protection needed is the only protection available, namely, Christ Himself. Here is an extract of the prayer:

---

that speech will help you save your situation. You must be alert at all times to let others know what is happening to you. You must use your brain and your voice any time that any work of yours will help you or others. You are a tactical unit and you must think of yourself that way. Don't try to win a war or capture a hill all by yourself. Your action alone means nothing, or at best, very little. It is when you talk to others and they join with you that your action becomes important.' See S. L. A. Marshall, *Men against Fire: the Problem of Battle Command* (Norman: University of Oklahoma Press, 2012) p. 137.

31. To cultivate vigilance, we will need to think as much about how we end our day as how we begin it. The following ancient advice, passed along from a Greek philosopher through Samuel Johnson, is worth pondering: 'Let not sleep, says Pythagoras, fall upon thy eyes till thou hast thrice reviewed the transactions of the past day. Where have I turned aside from rectitude? What have I been doing? What have I left undone, which I ought to have done? Begin thus from the first act, and proceed; and in conclusion, at the ill which thou hast done be troubled, and rejoice for the good.' See Samuel Johnson, *The Rambler*, No. 8, 1750.

SURVIVING THE TRENCHES

I bind unto myself today
The power of God to hold and lead,
His eye to watch, His might to stay,
His ear to hearken to my need.
The wisdom of my God to teach,
His hand to guide, His shield to ward,
The word of God to give me speech,
His heavenly host to be my guard.

Against the demon snares of sin,
The vice that gives temptation force,
The natural lusts that war within,
The hostile men that mar my course;
Or few or many, far or nigh,
In every place and in all hours,
Against their fierce hostility,
I bind to me these holy powers.

Against all Satan's spells and wiles,
Against false words of heresy,
Against the knowledge that defiles,
Against the heart's idolatry,
Against the wizard's evil craft,
Against the death wound and the burning,
The choking wave and the poisoned shaft,
Protect me, Christ, till Thy returning.

Christ be with me, Christ within me,
Christ behind me, Christ before me,
Christ beside me, Christ to win me,
Christ to comfort and restore me.[32]

---

32. For full prayer see https://www.prayerfoundation.org/st_patricks_breastplate_prayer.htm Accessed November 2021.

3

How to Kill an Entrenched Passion

◁◁◁♦♦♦▷▷▷

Pause and consider a question. If I asked you, 'How do you kill an evil passion?' what would you say? Most Christian men that I meet with respond with two words: prayer and repentance. At one level these are good answers – even right answers. However, they are suspiciously deficient in a way that many Sunday school responses are. Technically, they pin the tail on the donkey, but practically, they don't offer enough information to be useful. The reply assumes two things: (1) that men know what genuine repentance entails and (2) that men understand what earnest engagement with God looks like. My experience is that these are big assumptions to make. Repentance is easily confused with a phony apology. Likewise, confession is often mistaken for a robotic 'I'm sorry' that sounds more like a magic password than an act of contrition. What, then, is the answer to the question? How does a person kill an evil passion? The answer is indeed prayer and repentance; however – like two carefully packed suitcases – there is a lot more stuffed into these words than some would like to think.

It's worth looking at the same problem from a different angle. I was recently discussing with a group of men a very good book on battling pornography called *Finally Free* by Heath Lambert. One of the chapters is entitled 'Using Sorrow to Fight Pornography.' In this chapter he helpfully distinguishes the difference between 'worldly sorrow' and 'godly sorrow.' The one is me-saturated. All of the shame and guilt orbits around the weight of the self.[1] The other is God-centered; it is a sorrow like that of David which confesses, 'Against you, you only, have I sinned' (Ps. 51:4). The chapter is gold. I would happily print off copies and hand them out to every Christian man that I know. Yet, at the same time, the chapter is incomplete. There is one dilemma that Lambert uncovers (indirectly), but never resolves. It is this: what does a Christian man do if he does not have godly sorrow? This is not a theoretical problem. The core of sin is misdirected desire, loving something that is unworthy of our affection, or loving something in a way that is unworthy of true love. The lustful man, for instance, objectifies women for one reason: because he enjoys objectifying them. If there was no pleasure in the deed, he would not do it.

This creates a sticky problem for Christians entangled in sin. What should we do when we know that we ought to feel remorse for something, but in fact, do not? Every honest man can identify with the predicament. Repenting is straightforward when we hate our sin and long to be liberated from it. Yet, what about the all-too-common moments when we find enjoyment in appeasing a sinful appetite? What do we do when gluttony, or selfish ambition, is a mistress that we long to lie in bed with? How should we react when our prayers are stoic and our repentance mechanical? Although these circumstances might be extreme, they are not unusual. This numbness is a common effect of sin. Like a virus, sin infiltrates the heart, using our God-given design against us. One of the first things to be perverted is our moral vision. We no longer think straight; we no longer see straight; we no longer feel straight. The heart is subtly turned inside out so that evil begins to look (and feel) good, and good, evil.

---

1. See Heath Lambert, *Finally Free: Fighting for Purity with the Power of Grace* (Grand Rapids: Zondervan, 2013), pp. 31-45.

HOW TO KILL AN ENTRENCHED PASSION

We need to feel the tension of this condition. If sin is felt to be a small problem, a slight drifting out of lane which is easily corrected by a turn of the wheel, then the process of killing sin will be trivialized. We will march against sin with the naivety of so many generals who have led armies into Afghanistan thinking to themselves, 'This will be a short and easy fight.' This is precisely what happens with most men. They think that prayer and repentance are like salt and pepper: just a sprinkle of each is all that is needed to do away with sin. Sadly, this is not the case. For habituated sin, the deep passions and patterns of behavior that have hardened over years, a more arduous path is usually required to arrive at the crest of freedom. Yes, godly sorrow is indeed a remedy to such sins, but getting there – finding one's way to the place of genuine confession – often takes more time and requires more labor than a lot of Christians are willing to admit.[2]

The purpose of this chapter is to chart the long road that needs to be followed when sinful desires are deeply entrenched in the heart. This road will be marked by four stages: detect, reflect, reject, and correct. It is important to note that I am intentionally using the word 'stage' rather than 'step.' A four-step plan would betray a fundamental premise of this chapter. It would give the sense that repentance is a quick motion that the well-practiced spiritual athlete can perform with ease. This is not the case. Repentance often feels like siege warfare. The process can be slow – *painfully slow*. Often weeks, months, even years can pass before any progress is felt or seen. Yet, this should not dishearten us.

---

2. John Owen says, 'Most men love to hear the doctrine of grace, of the pardon of sin, of God's free love for His people, and suppose they find food therein; however, it is evident that they grow and thrive in the life and notion of them. But to be breaking up the fallow ground of their hearts, to be inquiring after the weeds and briers that grow in them, they delight not so much – though this be no less necessary than the other. This path is not so beaten as that of grace, nor so trod in, though it is the only way to come to a true knowledge of grace itself.' See *Indwelling Sin in a Believer* (Kindle edition).

As any mature Christian knows, God's priorities are rarely speed and efficiency. The same God who designed trees designed us. There is a lesson in this. Our Heavenly Father cares a lot more about the health of our roots and the strength of our core than about the time it takes for us to attain full stature. Keeping this in mind, we should not be surprised if the fruits of repentance take a while to bud and ripen.

Now, this chapter needs to be read from a particular point of view. It would be easy to interpret what is written as if what follows is a man-made strategy for defeating sin – as if there is some method that in and of itself has the power to dispel evil desire. I cannot reject this idea too forcefully.[3] There is only one person who can kill sin. His name is not Tom, Dick, or Harry. His name is the Holy Spirit. Likewise, there is only one power that can pull up a sin by its roots. This power is not 'fortitude,' or 'grit,' or 'resolve.' It is the power of grace. Thus, the difficulty of repentance is more than anything else the difficulty of humility. How do we reach a posture of brokenness before the Throne of Grace? This is our only position of strength against sin. If we can get there, the might of heaven is on our side. But getting there – that is the challenge.[4]

Stage 1: Detect – Build Awareness

This stage may seem obvious, as if it does not need individual treatment. Such prejudice needs to be put aside. There is nothing simple or easy about detecting sin. There are two main reasons for this.

The first is that most Christians have spent very little time analyzing either sinful or godly passions. Spiritual passions don't receive the treatment that they deserve in churches, and they certainly do not find

---

3. John Owen warns, 'Mortification from a self-strength, carried on by ways of self-invention, unto the end of a self-righteousness, is the soul and substance of all false religion in the world.' See *The Mortification of Sin* (Kindle edition).

4. Andrew Murray says, 'Just as water ever seeks and fills the lowest place, so the moment God finds you abased and empty, His glory and power flow in.' See *Humility* (Kindle edition).

their way into any common curriculum.[5] As a result of this neglect, even after years of being members in churches, most men know very little about the mechanics of envy, lust, or greed. Men are more adept at reading the moods of the atmosphere than the moods of their hearts.

Such ignorance is a major obstacle for detecting sin. At times, sinful outbursts of passion are like geysers – unmistakable for their violence and destructive force. Most of us do not need a visit by an angel to inform us that there is a problem after we have lost our temper and made a child cry, or when we've finally shut down the web browser after looking at porn. Yet, for every busted pipe that floods the heart, there will be any number of slight leaks that never get noticed. It is often these more subtle drips that over time cause the greatest damage.

It is worth taking a moment to ask what a man should do to overcome this deficiency. The quick answer is that he needs to make spiritual passions – the good, the bad, and the ugly – a special topic of study.[6] Before going to war, a general will study whatever intel reports are available on an enemy. The more he knows about the opponent, the more easily he can counter him. The same rule is true for spiritual combat. There is a myth that sin is unique, novel, and infinitely complex. We sometimes think that our struggle is so different from everyone else's that there is no help to be found outside of ourselves.

---

5. For a classic book on the topic, see Isaac Watts, *The Doctrines of the Passions Explained and Improved*. For a more recent work on the topic, see Robert Solomon, *The Passions: Emotions and the Meaning of Life* (Cambridge: Hackett, 1993).

6. John Owen says, 'To labour to be acquainted with the ways, wiles, methods, advantages, and occasions of its *success*, is the beginning of this warfare.' Elsewhere he adds, 'And, indeed, one of the choicest and most eminent parts of practically spiritual wisdom consists in finding out the subtleties, policies, and depths of any indwelling sin; to consider and know wherein its greatest strength lies, – what advantage it uses to make of occasions, opportunities, temptations, – what are its pleas, pretenses, reasonings, – what its stratagems, colours, excuses; to set the wisdom of the Spirit against the craft of the *old man*.' See *The Mortification of Sin* (Kindle edition).

This is the propaganda of Satan. Sin is not unique, novel, and infinitely complex; it is generic, commonplace, and boring. On this point, C. S. Lewis writes, 'How monotonously alike all the great tyrants and conquerors have been: how gloriously different the saints.'[7] We should not imagine sin to be a virus that constantly mutates and adapts such that the remedies of the past are of no use today. The opposite is true: The mechanics of pride, lust, and anger have not changed much over the centuries. The vanity and competitive spirit that plagued the Corinthians 2,000 years ago is the same vanity and competitive spirit that wrecks Christian communities today.

For our purposes, this is good news. It means that we can learn a lot about our own struggle against sin by listening to the collected wisdom of Christians who went before us. Both by reading classic works on sin and by developing an appetite for Christian literature and art, men can develop a working profile of the deadly passions. This knowledge will be exceedingly helpful for identifying their presence and monitoring their movements. As Sun Tzu said long ago, there is nothing more basic to the art of war than *knowing your enemy*.

The second reason sin is difficult to detect is because most men suffer from a lack of self-awareness. Self-awareness is a dangerous topic. We live in an age of narcissism in which every podcast is telling us to pay more attention to ourselves. The risk of this should be obvious. Vanity and pride graze on nothing more happily than staring too long in the mirror. Yet, this slippery slope does not eliminate the need for men to keep an eye on the motions of their hearts. A lot of men are blind slaves to their passions. This passivity plays right into the hand of the devil. John Bunyan wrote a fascinating allegory called *Holy War*. The book is

---

7. Chesterton demonstrates the same truth in his Father Brown stories. The only reason why a humble priest is able to solve crimes is because, having sat in the confession box for years, he is well acquainted with the ruts of the criminal mind. *Mere Christianity* (New York: Touchstone, 1996), p. 190.

about Mansoul, a city that Shaddai built for Himself, but that Diabolus seeks to capture and enslave. Originally, when Shaddai built the city, he installed Lord Understanding as mayor. All passions were intended to be under his authority. Yet, after Diabolus gains entry into the city, one of his first moves is to fire Lord Understanding, to throw him in a dark prison, and to hire Lord Lusting to fill the vacant chair.

The point that Bunyan was making is not difficult to see. One of the chief strategies of sin is to demote the mind to menial work while promoting unrestrained passion to the position of CEO. Once this happens, men relinquish the reigns of self-control. Functionally, they become slaves of their own erratic desires. Action follows passion like thunder follows lightning. There is no safeguard, or check, to buffer between anger and abuse, between lust and fornication, or between envy and slander.[8]

In order to break this chain, men must grow in a spiritual form of self-awareness. Just as an experienced mechanic can listen to the sound of an engine and tell if the timing is off, so a mature Christian needs to be able to hear the tremors of pride or of anger rumbling in the heart. Most of us can already do something similar to this with regard to our physical health. We have sufficient experience with illness to be able to diagnose the symptoms of a common cold, or the flu, or a bacterial infection like Strep Throat. We ought to have a similar working knowledge of spiritual health. We ought to be as quick to spot the odor of gluttony or sloth as we are to register a sore throat or a stuffy nose.

A concrete example will further illustrate the need for observing the motions of the heart. Picture two Christian men, Jim and Steve. They graduated from the same high school and are attending the

---

8. Two helpful treatments of the process by which habit enchains the will are Samuel Johnson's *The Vision of Theodore, the Hermit of Teneriffe, Found in His Cell* and Thomas Chalmers' *On the Power, Wisdom, and Goodness of God* (see section 1.3). Digital copies are available for both online.

same twenty-year reunion. From the moment that Jim walks into the event, he is plagued by a feeling that simmers just beneath the brim of consciousness. For weeks he has been dreading the event. Now that he is finally mingling among old peers, an unregistered heart-monitor is beeping. He is incessantly measuring his own success and happiness by the perceived success and happiness of others. One friend has a more exciting career than he does; another a prettier wife; another more accomplished children; another a fancier car; another public accolades for serving in the military; and so the pattern repeats. Feelings of envy, status-anxiety, vanity, and pride ebb and flow through the inner recesses of Jim's heart like waves on a seashore. Yet, none of this is consciously observed, much less combatted. Instead, these feelings are like a white-noise in the background of his soul, a sound that he hears and even responds to without having any awareness of what is going on.

Steve is also at the event. All of the same passions surge repeatedly within his heart, but instead of being passive, he relentlessly keeps an eye on what is going on. Like an air traffic controller, his eyes diligently scan all corners of his heart for suspicious activity. Thus, when envy surfaces, it is immediately identified and labeled.[9] Likewise, vanity is pinpointed before it can slip in under the radar. A spotlight is cast on pride before it has time to land in the dark. It is important to reiterate that what separates Jim and Steve is not a difference in feelings. The attack is no less severe for Steve than it is for Jim. The important difference between the men is this: whereas Jim is ignorant of what is going on and therefore defenseless against assault, Steve knows something about the position and formation of the enemy. At

---

9. Labeling something is a powerful way of rejecting something. Neil Postman refers to this as the label-libel rule. It's one thing to harbor an unidentified feeling of resentment. It's something else to name this feeling, envy. The mere label of 'envy' carries a sting of guilt with it. For the label-libel rule see Neil Postman, *Teaching as a Subversive Activity* (New York: Delta, 1971).

a minimum, he is aware that a battle is at hand and that his soul must prepare itself to make a defensive stand.

As Christians, we don't have the option to be pacifists in the war against sin. We cannot opt out of the battle. This leaves only three options on the table: ignorance, indifference, or alertness. Alertness is not the end of the battle against sin; it is the beginning. This is why detecting sin is no small feat. It is the trumpet blast that announces an ambush has begun.

Stage 2: Reflect – Get Sanity

Noticing an enemy on the horizon is not the same thing as defeating an enemy. By the time that the Greeks were burning down the mansions of Troy, every citizen in the city was perfectly aware that a war was going on. Yet, such knowledge did nothing to keep the city from being razed to the ground. Something similar is true of sin. Detecting and combating are not the same. Therefore, we cannot sit back contentedly after recognizing the problem. We must move on quickly to the next stage of repentance.

Now, in order to do justice to the battle against sin, we must picture two types of warfare occurring in the heart. One type is like a sudden skirmish. Unexpectedly, sin attacks like a guerrilla army hiding at a bend in a road. Every Christian can attest to feeling a rush of greed or of gluttony that was startling and noteworthy precisely because it felt out of character. The battle against sin is sometimes like this. Old passions lie dormant for years, even decades, and then erupt with the sudden force of Mount St. Helens. The best tactics to use against such outbursts are swift movements of offensive strength: a forceful rejection of temptation, sincere petitions to God for strength and mercy, and, as needed, honest confession to a mature and trustworthy friend. Often such defenses are sufficient to dissolve the insurgent force of a passion.

But there is another type of battle against sin that is more aligned with the focus of this chapter. Often as we begin to observe our hearts, we come across encampments of sin that are deeply entrenched and heavily fortified. We discover that pride, or sloth, has built a castle within the heart, one that has been organizing, coordinating, and directing the more sporadic skirmishes that have assaulted us. Slowly, we begin to realize that all of the minor contests with sinful desire have not been random or disconnected. Instead, we come to see that there is a stronghold of sin in the heart, one that must be confronted, demolished, and removed if we are to enjoy any lasting peace and freedom.

Still, discovering a stronghold and truly understanding it are two different things. This is where the analogy of sin inhabiting a castle breaks down. Once a castle is spotted, its structure and size are relatively clear. A commanding general knows with a degree of accuracy what he is up against. Consequently, he can begin to strategize how to mobilize his forces to destroy the fortification.

The ramparts of sin are not so obvious. Locating the root of sin is more like searching for the inner network of a terrorist cell than identifying the citadel at the top of a castle. This is part of why killing sin – especially deeply entrenched sin – is so difficult. Most of the time we are not quite sure what we are up against. Do we see patterns? Yes. Can we trace these patterns back to a central problem? This is where extra work is required.

At this point using an example will be more insightful than speaking generally. Therefore, let's pick up the case of Steve who was mentioned above.

Steve, as has been noted already, keeps a careful eye on the motions of his heart. As a result of this attentiveness, for some time he has been aware that pride has a commanding influence on his feelings, actions, and desires. Yet, the more he thinks about the problem, the more the diagnosis 'pride' seems too generic to be useful. Although the label might specify the trunk of what is growing within his heart, further digging is required to uncover the deeper and more specific roots that underlie the problem.

Taking this into consideration, Steve decides to prayerfully reflect on the hidden nature of his struggle. Daily he speaks to God, 'Search me, O God, and know my heart! Try me and know my thoughts! And see if there be any grievous way in me' (Ps. 139:23-24). In addition, as he prays, he begins to take notes in his prayer journal whenever a new aspect of his pride is spotted. On a quiet afternoon he does something else that may, to some, look a little obsessive: He takes a few minutes to organize his thoughts and to mind-map his discoveries, tracing previously unseen connections between the deep channel of pride and its lesser tributaries.

Through these efforts, a work that goes on for many weeks, a clearer picture slowly emerges. Instead of only recognizing the trunk, pride, he begins to disentangle the roots that feed and enlarge this trunk. He sees that his pride is not just one solid thing – like a large hunk of granite. Rather, it is a network of interrelated desires. As he pulls these roots apart, he begins to name them: an implacable desire for social visibility, a need for peer recognition, a lust for popular praise, an impassioned urge to be remembered, and a tightly guarded craving to define his own legacy. All of these are as closely connected to pride as the lungs and heart are connected to the circulatory system. Moreover, he begins to realize that unless these roots are cut off, no matter how many branches he trims, the trunk will continue to thicken and grow.

As weeks continue to pass, Steve's self-analysis yields a second fruit. He begins to understand, not just the roots of his sin, but the soil that feeds these roots. Sinful passions never grow in a vacuum. Rather, they always depend on a bed of lies to be nourished. As Steve starts to see this, in the same notebook where he has been logging the roots of pride, he also now jots down whatever sediment of unbelief is uncovered. It does not take long for Steve to create a list of sinister lies that have settled in his heart. These lies are more felt to be true than actively professed to be true. The list includes the following: the belief that God's love is not sufficient to give him worth and dignity; the belief that God's will for his life is not good – or good enough; the belief that his labor is in vain and does not amount to anything significant; the belief that no one is watching – not even God; and finally, the belief that the approval and praise of people matters more than the love and acceptance of God. As Steve writes these lies down, his conscience is pricked by shame. He knows that none of these statements is true, and yet - here he breathes a sigh of frustration – *and yet* somehow such lies have poisoned the bloodstream of his worship.

Steve's Notebook	
The Roots of Desire	The Soil of Lies
Lust for social visibility	Your love and acceptance is not enough
Lust for peer recognition	Your will is not good
Lust for popular praise	No one sees my labor
Lust to be remembered	Jesus is not enough of an audience
Lust to fulfill self-defined dreams	

And so, the process goes on for several months. Then, after much prayer, reflection, and self-observation, Steve looks down at his notepad one day and has a eureka moment. 'That's it!' he says to himself. As he looks down at the paper in front of him, he realizes that the clouds of ambiguity have all but receded. He knows that – finally – he has a clear and accurate diagnosis. For the first time, the pieces fit together so that the puzzle of his pride is seen for what it is – soil, root, trunk and leaves.[10] On the one hand, this brings Steve a sense of relief. He now

---

10. It is worth noting that there is often a kernel of righteousness covered over by the outer crust of sin. Selfish ambition is a good example of this. There is

feels like the mask hiding his sin has been ripped off. On the other, a touch of anguish twinges his heart. More clearly than ever before, he sees that this is no small tree that needs to be felled. It is an old and gnarly oak whose roots are as wide and expansive as are its branches.

Clarity and accuracy: These are the two key objectives of stage two for fighting sin, the stage we have labeled 'reflect.' It is important for men to realize just how crucial this stage is for battling deeply entrenched passions. Too often men do not know who the enemy is or where he is hiding. As a result of this ignorance, the best they can do is to drop bombs at random, hoping that something hits an enemy bunker. This is how most confession works. Men very generally apologize to God for sins that are ambiguous and barely understood. They may confess their anger, for example, but never see the connection between an underlying attitude of entitlement and the wrath it produces. They may be frustrated by their gluttony, but they never see the sloth that creates the empty hole that gluttony is trying to fill.

There is a better way to go about warring against sin. If the position of the enemy is known and carefully marked, rather than firing at random, a person can strike strategically. He can confess before God with precision, both requesting specific forgiveness for specific sins and requesting specific mercy for specific needs. This clear and accurate line of communication is a vital resource in the battle against entrenched desire.

Stage 3: Reject – Tap into a Deeper Love

To understand what is required to reject a sin, we need to remember the fundamental difficulty of sin. One of sin's chief powers is to distort our vision so that evil looks good and good, evil. The classic example

---

something good about not wanting to waste the gift of life. However, this deep desire can easily be bent out of shape by pride. Men need to be careful lest they attempt to squash a seed of righteousness while mortifying sin.

of this is Eve in the garden. Why did she eat the forbidden fruit? The answer is plain – it looked good.[11] Her moral vision was skewed so that what ought to have been an object of fear was instead an object of desire. The same process occurs time and again. Whether we are talking about anger or gluttony, greed or lust, the effect of each passion is the same. It filters our vision so that the darkness appears vibrant and colorful and the light, dull and insipid.

This distortion creates a nettlesome problem. No one has explained the problem more succinctly than Jesus. In the Sermon on the Mount He says, 'The eye is the lamp of the body. So, if your eye is healthy, your whole body will be full of light, but if your eye is bad, your whole body will be full of darkness. If the light that is in you is darkness, how great is the darkness!' (Matt. 6:22-23). Packed neatly in this saying is a profound truth: If we cannot see differently, we cannot love differently; if we cannot love differently, we cannot desire differently; and if we cannot desire differently, we cannot choose differently. Herein lies the bondage of sin. Sin casts a spell over the heart that confuses the goodness of the good and the evilness of evil. We wind up guilty of the charge leveled by Isaiah:

> *Woe to those who call evil good*
> *and good evil,*
> *who put darkness for light*
> *and light for darkness,*
> *who put bitter for sweet*
> *and sweet for bitter!* (Isa. 5:20).

Now, breaking this spell is not easy work. It can only be accomplished by doing two things.

The first is to meditate on the evil, danger, guilt, and shame of sin. However, the idea of meditating on sin might be an eccentric thought

---

11. The same pattern is evident in the sins of Achan (Josh. 7), David (2 Sam. 11), and Gehazi (2 Kings 5) among other examples.

to many. To some, it may even sound perverse.[12] However, the exercise is important for the following reason: We will never seek to kill sin until we hate sin, and we will never hate sin until we see sin for what it truly is. The best way to stir up such holy hatred is by interrogating an evil passion to discover its actual nature and ultimate agenda.

At this point it is useful to return to the case study of Steve. Recall the results of Steve's reflection. On the upside, he gained clarity. On the downside, reflection did nothing to loosen the roots of sin. The strength of sin is not diminished through diagnosis. Self-awareness can identify a weed, but it cannot pull one out.

Realizing this, Steve begins to add an element to his daily devotion. He allots a few minutes each morning to dissecting the true nature of his pride. This often takes the form of an inquisition. He asks pointed questions to expose the evil of self-centeredness. These include questions like the following: 'What am I really desiring when I desperately seek praise and self-advancement?' 'What do these aspirations reveal about the deep worship of my heart?' 'What do my longings for achievement indicate about the status of Christ in my life?'

One day during his quiet time, Steve reads Colossians 1:18 where Paul says that the rightful position of Christ is preeminence over everything. This truth rattles Steve's heart. In a flash of insight, he

---

12. By advising men to meditate on their sin, I am not advising them to meditate on the self. The goal of this exercise is not self-loathing, but sin-loathing. The goal is to see evil for what it is. Heath Lambert warns of the danger of mental punishments. He says, 'Mental punishments are not helpful because they deal with sin in a self-centered way instead of a Christ-centered way. Meditating on how miserable and pathetic you are only perpetuates the sinful self-centeredness that led you to look at pornography in the first place. Condemning self-talk still has you standing center stage as you reflect on what you think you deserve because of what you did…. The only way to break this vicious cycle is to get outside of yourself to Jesus. You need to stop talking to yourself in categories of condemnation and begin talking to God in categories of confession.' The same advice applies to other sins besides pornography. See Heath Lambert, *Finally Free*, p. 26.

sees the essence of his pride. He realizes – as hideous as it is to say aloud – that deep down there is a wish within him that Christ could be demoted so that he could take a turn sitting at the right hand of God.[13] This realization does not just startle Steve; it horrifies him. He is made aware of a brewing tension within his soul. On the one hand, the flesh is warring against the Spirit. His pride is tugging him toward the desire to usurp the preeminence of Christ. On the other, the Spirit is warring against the flesh. Beneath the pride is a genuine love of Jesus that longs for nothing more than the day when every knee shall bow and tongue confess that Christ is lord.

As this occurs, unbeknownst to Steve, something else is happening in his heart. One effect of seeing more clearly the ugliness of sin is that the shine of pride is diminished by a degree. Although the magic of the passion has not yet been broken, there is reason to be encouraged: Its force is waning.

Similarly, in times of prayer, Steve also begins to consider the danger of his pride. He asks himself, 'What would happen if God handed me over completely to my desires for acclaim, prestige, recognition, and success?' It does not take long for the thought experiment to produce terrifying results. Steve pictures the man he would become if pride were installed as absolute monarch of the soul. He imagines the effect this would have on his marriage, on his children, on his friendships. There is nothing appealing about becoming a thoroughgoing narcissist. Misery and loneliness – this is the home that pride would purchase for him.

Yet, the experiment does not end there. Having studied Romans 8:7, Steve knows that the core of all sin is hatred of God. Therefore, as he continues to trace the trajectory of unrestrained pride, he sees that, ultimately, if pride were not mitigated by grace, it would lead him – not

---

13. C. J. Mahaney talks about how relabeling sin can increase conviction of sin. His personal example is renaming pride 'contending with the supremacy of God.' See C. J. Mahaney, *Humility: True Greatness*.

just to the threshold of Hell – but across the doorstep, down the stairwell, and into the basement of eternal separation from God.[14] This line of meditation reinforces the impact of the earlier one. The charm of sin continues to disintegrate as the wages of sin are counted for what they are.

Steve's Notebook	
The Evil of Pride	The Danger of Pride
I want to be worshiped	Pride redirects my worship
I scorn the dignity of my adoption	Pride generates anxiety
I am dissatisfied with my calling	Pride deifies the self
I care more about people than God	Pride cancels love
I look to success to give me happiness	Pride blunts usefulness for the kingdom
I use other people to judge my worth	Pride silences prayer

On other days, Steve explores similar lines of thought, considering the shame and guilt of pride.[15] First, regarding shame, he reminds himself of the original design of human beings. He thinks about the way in which we were made, not to grasp for power and position, but to serve and love one another. Pride, he concludes, is a perversion of the beauty and dignity of our design. It is an imitation of Satan, not an imitation

---

14. Anthony DeStefano writes, 'The greatest spiritual writers of all time and from every tradition in Christianity agree on one essential point regarding hell: the most intense pain and the chief punishment suffered by the souls of the damned is their eternal separation and self-exclusion from God. God made humans possess the kind of happiness they truly desire. If a soul loses the ability to be in union with God, it essentially loses everything.' See Anthony DeStefano, *Hell: A Guide* (Nashville: Thomas Nelson, 2020) p. 64.

15. John Owen discusses just how important it is to load the conscience with the guilt of sin. He says, 'If ever thou wilt mortify thy corruptions, thou must tie up thy conscience to the law, shut it from all shifts and exceptions, until it owns its guilt with a clear and thorough apprehension.' He adds, 'Unless this be done to the purpose, all other endeavors are to no purpose. Whilst the conscience hath any means to alleviate the guilt of sin, the soul will never vigorously attempt its mortification.' See *The Mortification of Sin* (Kindle edition).

of God. The thought of growing in the likeness of Satan is sobering. Once again, the appeal of pride is dampened.

Furthermore, Steve weighs the guilt of pride using the law of God. He knows that the first and the greatest commandment is to love God with heart, mind, soul, and strength (cf. Matt. 22:36-40). This commandment adjusts Steve's thinking. Often, in the past, pride has felt like a slight misdemeanor to Steve. He has reckoned that, because everyone struggles with pride, pride must not be too grievous of an offense. Yet, set beside the first commandment, the penny drops that pride is not like a parking ticket, a small fine easily paid; it is more akin to an act of treason, something that calls for decisive and merciless punishment. He sees that pride shatters the most sacred and fundamental law of the entire universe – the commandment that all glory and praise be directed to God (cf. Isa. 42:8, 1 Cor. 15:28). As this truth slowly sinks into Steve's consciousness, a new feeling arises. He begins to feel dirty. There is a stain in the heart that needs to be purged.

Now stepping back from this case study, the point needs to be reiterated that such meditation is not the work of a single afternoon. It is fruit of regular, ongoing, and patient contemplation. Sadly, a lot of men will not be willing to do this, which is why the attractive power of sin will persist in spite of their confession. One half of their heart will ask forgiveness of God while the other half secretly longs to go back to the poisoned well and drink again. Men need to realize that there is no way to kill sin without confronting desire. It will only be after the sinfulness of sin is acutely felt that we will find ourselves pleading with God to rescue us from the chains of evil passion.[16]

Yet, hatred of sin is not sufficient in and of itself to break the spell of sin. For this, love of holiness is required. A lot of Christian men

---

16. A good litmus test is whether or not a person can pray through Psalm 51 with any sincerity.

second guess whether or not they truly love God. They mistake feeling for reality. Thus, if they don't feel warm and buttery emotions, they assume that love is not there. Yet, the truth is this: If a person is a Christian, then the bedrock of his soul is love of God. We know this because Paul says, 'God's love has been poured out into our hearts through the Holy Spirit who has been given to us' (Rom. 5:5).[17]

Now the effect of sin is not to remove this deep layer of love. Sin has no power to do this. Instead, what sin does is bury this bedrock with layers of silt and refuse. This means that one of the primary tasks of deep repentance is to drill through these superficial layers of desire and pleasure in order to uncover the substratum of the heart. A true child of God can be assured that his first love does not disappear. This is why we can always return to the wells of our salvation (cf. Isa. 12:3). The challenge of repentance is tapping back into this subterranean stream after the soft flesh of the heart has been hardened through rebellion and self-indulgence.

So, how do we do this? The answer is not by meditating on sin, but meditating on God. It is only by remembering and cherishing the goodness of God that the crust of sin begins to crack and streams of living water begin to work their way back to the surface of the heart.

To see what this looks like, we need to focus back in on Steve. When we left him, he was just starting to be disgusted by the horror of sin. Instead of mistaking darkness for light, he was beginning to see just how dark the darkness really is. While such work is necessary, it is also incomplete. Something vital had not yet happened to Steve. Namely, he had not yet been reminded of the beauty and goodness of the light itself. It is one thing to be aware of the pitch blackness of a cavernous

---

17. Commentators debate whether the love mentioned in this verse is the love that we have for God or the love that God has for us. In truth, it is both. God's love is poured into us through the Holy Spirit, who then recirculates that love through our hearts and back to God. An endless cycle thus results of receiving and giving love.

cell. It is something else to compare this darkness with the splendor and beauty of a sunlit meadow.[18]

And so, Steve's battle continues. Having reached conviction regarding the evil and danger of his pride, he now turns his mind elsewhere. He starts to focus his meditation on the love of the Father, on the faithfulness of the Son, and on the indwelling presence of the Spirit. As he does this, he begins to feel the embers of spiritual love stoked and fanned.[19] The more time he takes to think about the kindness of his heavenly Father, the more bitter his independent spirit begins to taste. The more conscious he is that the Spirit grieves in the presence of evil, the more reluctant he is to harbor feelings of selfish ambition and envy. Yet, more than anything else, it is the cross that melts the granite of his heart. The closer he gets to the blazing love of Jesus, the more he experiences the truth of Isaac Watts' greatest hymn, 'When I Survey:'

> When I survey the wondrous cross
> On which the Prince of glory died
> My richest gain I count but loss
> And pour contempt on all my pride.

Yes, it is the form of Christ – the humility of His incarnation, the self-giving spirit of His ministry, and the unflinching submission of Calvary – that finally shatters the ramparts of sin and leaves the heart broken and laid bare before God. The more Steve gazes on Jesus, the

---

18. Thomas Watson says, 'The reason our affections are so cold to heavenly things is because we do not warm them at the fire of holy meditation. As the musing on amorous objects makes the fire of lust burn; the musings on injuries makes the fire of revenge burn; so meditating on the transcendent beauties of Christ, would make our love to Christ flame forth.' See *The Christian Soldier* (Kindle edition). Likewise, John Owen says, 'Fill your affections with the cross of Christ so that there may be no room for sin.' See *Indwelling Sin in Believers* (Kindle edition).

19. Note John Owen's insight: 'Longing, breathing, and panting after deliverance is a grace in itself, that hath a mighty power to conform the soul into the likeness of the thing longed after.' See *The Mortification of Sin* (Kindle edition).

more vehemently he longs that Christ would fulfill the ministry of Isaiah 61 on his behalf:

> *The Spirit of the Lord God is upon me,*
> *because the Lord has anointed me*
> *to bring good news to the poor;*
> *he has sent me to bind up the brokenhearted,*
> *to proclaim liberty to the captives,*
> *and the opening of the prison to those who are bound* (1-2).

This is the breakthrough for which all of the other work has been mere preparation. Finally, as Steve kneels in the presence of Jesus, tears melt from his eyes. He is no longer thinking about sin. He is now mourning and weeping over sin. His heart is a bonfire of spiritual emotion. He feels angry for the way in which sin has been deceiving him and luring him away from the arms of his beloved. He fervently longs to be rescued from the weakness of his flesh. He fears lest pride would cause him to miss out on the sweet communion that comes through walking closely with God. There is zeal to be cleared of the dishonor of sin, a mournful cry that God would shatter his pride like He broke the chariots of Pharaoh at the Red Sea.

And only now, after a long and tedious journey, is Steve's heart supple with contrition. The spell of sin is finally broken. All of its charm is gone. His heart is now united in a single plea: *'Lord, rescue me from my pride!'*

If godly sorrow were easy to access, there would be no need for a prolonged period of reflection and meditation. A person could turn on zeal, indignation, longing, and contrition like light switches on a wall. But this is not the case. It is only after we begin to hate our sin and to recover our sanity that godly emotion catches flame. And this flame is an important sign. It indicates that finally we are ready to repent with sincerity, integrity, and love. [20]

---

20. In *The Doctrine of Repentance* Thomas Watson says, 'The Christian has a sufficient measure of sorrow when the love of sin is purged.'

This leads us to the central act of – not just rejecting sin – but mortifying sin. In the end it is only the grace of God that can deliver us from a deeply entrenched passion. This is why everything up until this point is preparatory work. The most we can do is to humble ourselves such that we break before the Throne of Grace. It is this posture – collapsing for mercy at the feet of Jesus – that is our position of strength in the battle against sin. As Paul knew so well, our strength is in our weakness. It is only after we have emptied ourselves of all fleshly hope that the rain of mercy can be collected in the soul.

Yet, contrition is not the only benefit of following this long path of repentance. There is also clarity. It is one thing to kneel before God and to confess a generic brand of pride. It is an entirely different experience to name an exhaustive list of lies and subsidiary passions in a spirit of genuine penitence. The first is like yelling 'Help!' but not knowing exactly what help is needed. The other is like yelling, 'Save me from *this bear*, from *this lion*, and from *this Philistine giant*!' Such particularity engenders a more authentic encounter with God.

Still, there is another good that comes through this prolonged process. This longer road of self-examination not only enables us to confess specifically; it also helps us to be more detailed in our requests for mercy. The point has been made more than once that we cannot kill sin unless we replace sin. This means that we should never be content to say, 'God, please take away my pride.' The prayer is incomplete. We are not specifying what we would like to fill the void of pride. A much better prayer is something like the following:

> Lord, make me willing to live a life of obscurity like Jesus; Father, become my sole audience so that, like Christ, I can live exclusively for You; God, help me to accept the perfect goodness of your will and to see that the very best way that I can serve you is by becoming the man that you made me to be.

There is a secret law of prayer that, the more specifically we ask, the more specifically we tend to get. This needs to be remembered when we visit the Throne of Grace. Why be content with a generic request like 'humility.' A better approach is to lay before the feet of Jesus a detailed and compelling profile of the servant we long to be.

Stage 4: Correct – Act on Faith

It's easy to imagine that after such repentance the clouds will burst and mercy will fall in a torrential outpouring. The heart will suddenly be so satisfied by God that sin will shrivel and virtue blossom in its place with the speed of a time-lapse camera. But to think this is naïve. More than likely the immediate outcome of deep and radical repentance is this: *nothing*. The sky doesn't change colors. A gust of wind doesn't blow a man off his feet. There are no confetti cannons or fireworks. Quite the opposite: The world looks and feels the same after such heartfelt repentance as it did before. Yet, this should not discourage us.

There is a memorable scene in C. S. Lewis' Narnia book, *Prince Caspian*. The Narnians are on the brink of a decisive and devastating defeat. The evil King Miraz has surrounded them and left them with little provision and ebbing strength. There is only one last hope for the dwarfs, centaurs, and talking animals – Susan's horn. The old promise, which many have come to doubt, is that if the horn is blown, help is on the way. And so, finally, with nothing else to try, a blast of the horn is sounded.

After this occurs nothing visibly changes for the Narnians. Aslan doesn't leap out from a closet. Fiery hailstones don't fall from the sky, turning the enemy camp into a heap of ashes. Everything looks identical to how it did before. And yet, for those who know the story, the promise is not in vain. Though unseen, new forces are at work. Help, indeed, is on the way.

This is a beautiful picture of the aftermath of repentance. Genuine confession rarely yields a quick and definite victory over sin. And yet the Scriptures are abundantly clear that the cry of the brokenhearted never goes unnoted.[21] We can always rest assured that 'The Lord is near to the brokenhearted and saves the crushed in spirit' (Ps. 34:18). In God's perfect timing, in God's perfect measure, help will be on the way.

This leads to a final question. Where does all of this end? After we have asked for mercy, are we done? Do we simply sit passively and wait on supernatural strength to quicken us like Sampson waiting for his hair to grow? The answer is, *'No.'* The spirit of trust is far more daring than this. While we wait on mercy, we do not sit still like a driver waiting for a tow truck. Rather, believing that grace is already on the way, we get busy doing all of the various things that God has already told us need to be done.

What are these things? They are all the ordinary means of fighting sin. They are habituating our minds to put on Christ (Rom. 13:14); resisting the first movements of sin (Rom. 6:12); sharpening our faculties so that they are weapons of righteousness (Rom. 6:13); eliminating any standing provision for sin (Rom. 13:14); being proactive to develop the habits of godliness (Rom. 6:16); putting to death the deeds of the body (Rom. 8:13), and so on and so forth. There is no shortage of direction in the Scriptures. Therefore, in the interim, while we wait for the salvation that only God can provide, we get moving on the path He has already set before us.[22]

---

21. See 1 Samuel 15:22; Psalm 34:18; Psalm 51:17; Psalm 147:3, Isaiah 57:15 among other references.

22. According to I John 2:15-16, the roots of sin are the desire of the flesh (gluttony), the desire of the eyes (greed), and the pride of life (pride). It is worth noting that the disciplines of Matthew 6 are practical ways of combatting these sinful passions. To practice generosity is to attack the roots of greed; to practice fasting is to attack the roots of gluttony; to practice prayer is to attack the roots of pride. For more on the way in which embodied disciplines are useful for reforming the heart, see Brant Pitre, *Introduction to the Spiritual Life: Walking the Path of Prayer and Discipleship with Jesus* (Image: New York, 2021), chapters 4-9.

Yet, there is one final thing that we can do in the midst of heated combat with sin. We can rejoice in suffering (Rom. 5:3; 8:18). Often, Christians think of suffering only in terms of social persecution or bodily illness. We forget that the remnants of sin plague our heart like arthritis plagues our limbs. Thus, we interpret our struggle against sin as a sign of failure. But this is not the case. Dead fish always swim with the tide. The only fish that resist the current are those which are living and active. The same is true of Christians. Though we may long for the fight against sin to end, the mere fact that we are fighting is a reason to rejoice. It is a sure sign that the Spirit of God is at work in our members to liberate us from the lingering forces of sin.

We can conclude by finishing the story of Steve. After reaching a place of broken dependence on God, what, then, does Steve do? He begins to reshape his life so that he can radically pursue humility. This involves a number of things. First, he changes his morning routine. For the foreseeable future, he decides to start each day by meditating on the beauty of Christ's submission in Philippians 2. This, he hopes, will help protect him from the twisted desires of pride. Second, he decides to find an accountability partner for his pride. He knows that many men use accountability partners for lust. Why not, he thinks, follow the same wisdom with regard to pride? Finally, Steve begins to take stock of his environment. He starts to see that his heart problem is fed by many triggers in the world around him. One of these influences is the ethic of achievement that dominates the culture of his workplace. This insight does not result in Steve changing jobs or careers. However, it does affect his daily mindset. He no longer views the office as a neutral space without spiritual significance. More than ever before, the following words of Jesus gird his mind: 'Behold, I am sending you out as sheep in the midst of wolves, so be wise as serpents and innocent as doves' (Matt. 10:16).

4

Four Sins That Are Killing Modern Men

◁◁◁♦♦♦▷▷▷

One of the difficulties with fighting sin is that there are two types of enemies that we face. Many men will have heard about the famous Carthaginian general named Hannibal who led his army – and a herd of elephants – over the Alps and into Italy. They may also be aware that Rome eventually defeated the Carthaginians and left their empire a pile of ashes. However, here is a fact that a lot of men will not have heard: After Hannibal invaded Italy, he spent fifteen years ravaging villages and towns in the peninsula. *Fifteen years!* That is a long time to have a known and feared enemy burning houses in the countryside. Some sin is like this. It is as obvious as a foreign army waving banners in the backyard. In such cases, the problem is not identifying sin, but eliminating sin. We know what needs to be repelled; we're just not sure how to defeat it.

Yet, other times the opponent is less visible. In Isaiah 39 there is a terrifying story in which King Hezekiah entertains a group of ambassadors from a distant kingdom called Babylon. After the envoys leave, the prophet Isaiah shows up and asks Hezekiah, 'Where did these men come from?' Unconcerned, Hezekiah tells the story. The ensuing words of Isaiah are chilling to read: 'Hear the word of the LORD of hosts: Behold, the days are coming, when all that is in your house, and that which your fathers have stored up till this day, shall be carried to Babylon. Nothing shall be left, says the Lord' (Isa. 39:5-6). The disturbing truth was that Hezekiah had spent his entire life so worried about the Assyrians that he had never taken time to consider that a more powerful threat could be coming from a different direction. He had no clue that the men he was wining and dining were heralds of a looming invasion.

Men need to know that a lot of passions do not rattle the soul like the treading of elephants. Instead, they slither in and out of small cracks in the heart unnoticed. This is why we can never put blind faith in our consciences. Just because we don't feel in danger does not mean that there is no venom in our blood. The final bar of righteousness is not how we feel, but what God says. It is God's blueprint, not our blood pressure, which determines the quality of the heart.

Now the purpose of this chapter is to bring the battle against sin into tighter focus. Ambiguity is always a spiritual liability. If we do not know what in particular to fight against, there is a good chance that the knowledge we've picked up thus far will rust in the shed of memory. I don't want this to happen. Therefore, to clear a path forward, in this chapter we will look closely at four passions that are wreaking havoc on the lives of modern men. Two of these passions are pride and lust. Like the elephants of Hannibal, they are well known and justly feared. Our difficulty with them is not so much ignorance as impotence. We struggle to believe that even small victories can be had against such belligerent aggression. The other two, vanity and sloth, are more obscure. They tend to operate like Babylon in the background of Isaiah – unidentified and thus ignored. Such passivity is exceedingly dangerous. Though the bite of vanity and sloth may be less deep than that of pride and lust, their venom is no less toxic. Left untreated, they, too, can kill.

Before considering these passions individually, it is worth taking a moment to consider what they have in common. All of them have the same effect on the heart: They distort and degrade the design of God. It is important to keep this idea of 'design' at the forefront of our minds as we reflect on these passions. The reason that these passions need to be avoided is not simply because they inspire trespasses against the laws of God – though they do indeed have this effect. At an even more basic level, these passions distort our design and degrade our dignity. Human beings – regardless of what the anthropologists say – are not built to be self-centered, to reduce each other to sexual objects, or to gorge ourselves to the point of incapacitation. We were made for love, respect, and service. The most profound evil of sinful passions is that they turn our nature inside out. They take what is good, twist it into something evil, and then use it for sin. There is one main truth that we need to glean from this. In discussing these passions, we will need to ask not only, 'What is wrong with each one?' but also 'What is right with each one?' In other words, we will need to think not only about the evil introduced by the passion, but also about the good that is being bent out of shape.

Target 1: Vanity[1]

John is a thirty-eight-year-old Christian man. He ends most days physically and mentally exhausted, having spent almost no time before God in prayer, Bible reading, or quiet reflection. Most nights he feels guilty about being lazy. The thought occurs to him that, if – after tucking in the kids to bed – he could just muster a final ounce of effort, he could read a chapter of the Bible before collapsing on the couch.

Yet a closer look at John's life might lead us to question whether laziness is the bottleneck restricting spiritual vigor. If someone were

---

1. Vanity is often confused with pride. Vanity here will refer to a social desire to fit into the empty values and practices of the world. Pride will refer to a deep self-centeredness and self-reliance that is fundamentally anti-social. The vain man is ultimately a people-pleaser. The proud man cares only to please himself.

to zoom out from narrowly observing John's life, he would see the following: Years ago John chose an especially demanding career, not to make a living or from a sense of calling, but in hopes of meeting the expectations of his parents and wider family. Four times a week he punishes himself for an hour in the gym, not to sustain health or to clear the mind, but because a thick chest wins bonus points in the office, and the time spent shuttling kids from sports practices to violin lessons is not driven by a desire to please God but the pressure to shoulder the merciless yoke of middle class America.

Now stand back and appraise the big picture. Is John lazy? Not at all. He is hardworking and goal-oriented, a virtuoso in getting things done. The leak in his heart is not idleness, but *vanity*. Vanity is driving him to pawn off peace, strength, and a close walk with God for nothing more than the ho-hum of *fitting in*.

Dissecting Vanity

Every human being has an in-built desire to be loved and found lovely by others.[2] God made us to be social animals. The validation that we do not just want, but need, is a gift that only other people can give us. I can stare in the mirror for as long as I want and repeat the mantra, 'I love myself,' but this will be to no avail. My heart – like your heart – will never be satisfied until someone else says, 'You are loved,' and grants me membership into their circle of belonging.

Now vanity is the passion that misdirects this deep, human need. Vanity is the impulse to purchase self-worth using the wrong standards and the wrong community. In truth, the love of God and our adoption into His family ought to be all that we need to secure the dignity and worth that we so deeply crave. Yet, the effect of vanity in the heart is

---

2. In *A Theory of Moral Sentiments* Adam Smith notes, 'The chief part of human happiness arises from the consciousness of being loved.' Smith's understanding of the social nature of human selfhood foreshadows a lot of more recent literature.

that we feel a deep insecurity about our net worth. Instead of trusting the voice of heaven, we use jobs, bank statements, cars and homes, resumes, the achievements of our children, and the reflection in the mirror to try to reinforce our fragile egos. We think that if we can just get into the right country club, or publish a book, or run a triathlon, that *then* we gain entry into some inner circle that will provide stability for the soul. Yet, none of this works. The more desperately we scavenge for identity, the less certain we are about where to find it.

Dr Seuss captures the comic nature of this search in a children's book about sneetches. At the start of the book, some sneetches have stars on their bellies; others do not. Those without stars suffer a sense of shame and degradation for not having them. Fortunately, one day a man shows up with a contraption that can put stars on bellies. Plain-bellied sneetches line up to pay whatever price is required in order to participate in what is considered to be a better brand of sneetch. Of course, this creates a social crisis. Once every sneetch has a star on his belly, there is no way to signal eliteness. Thus, a vicious cycle ensues of adding and removing stars, all for the sake of feeding vanity and protecting pride.

While the story is comic, the application is unnerving. The sad truth is that Christians are hardly better than non-Christians when it comes to wasting time, energy, and money trying to conform to the arbitrary values around us.[3] Think of the example of John mentioned above. How much of the stress and tiredness of his life is generated by nothing more than the effort to be a star-bellied sneetch? How much joyful fellowship with a loving God is sacrificed in order to garner the acceptance of a callous and indifferent world?

---

3. Anyone interested in thinking more deeply about how modern society educates vanity should peruse the following books: Alain de Botton, *Status Anxiety* (New York: Vintage, 2005) and Elizabeth Currid-Halkett, *The Sum of Small Things: a Theory of the Aspirational Class* (Princeton: PUP, 2018).

The Symptoms of Vanity

Vanity is endemic among modern men. Therefore, we need to be able to recognize the symptoms of the disease. There will be seasons when our identity is safely anchored by the love of God and our adoption in Christ. However, other times the winds of passion will begin to blow and our anchor will be unmoored. We need to be able to identify this quickly when it is happening. The following are telltale signs that a tempest of vanity is brewing in the soul.

One is discontentment. Driven by vanity, I feel like I am missing out, like there is some inner circle of people that I need to be included in. The lie of vanity is that by purchasing a new car, trimming body fat, earning a million dollars, or winning a corner office I can attain peace and security. However, vanity will no more allow for contentment than lust will allow for satisfaction. After one merit badge, there will always be another that I must earn in order to keep moving on the treadmill of acceptance.

A second is busyness. Vanity can never pursue a single aim because the world does not advertise a single good. To fit in, I must advance countless agendas at once. I must be a faithful member of my church, achieve fitness in the gym, experience the latest trends of pop culture, keep up the front yard to the standards of the neighborhood, grasp the next rung on the corporate ladder, and on and on and on. To be driven by vanity is to be thrown onto a circus stage and told to juggle a dozen pins at once. No man can bear such an exasperating load for long – at least not while pursuing a life of intimacy with God.[4]

A third is hypocrisy. There is the well-known saying, 'Fake it until you make it.' The problem with life is that many of the aspirations that we inherit from the world around us are impossible. No matter

---

4. David Brooks very helpfully shows how success is the true religion of America in *The Second Mountain: The Quest for the Moral Life* (New York: Random House, 2019), pp. 1-25.

how hard we try, we never will 'make it.' This leaves only one option on the table: faking it. Thus, vain people end up being hypocrites in the original sense of the word – they are actors wearing masks. They have to pretend to be something they are not because (sad to say) they are not what they pretend to be. This demonstrates why vanity always leads to misery. Vain people may fool the world, but they cannot fool themselves. At the end of the day, when the make-up comes off, the vain person must stare at his true reflection in the mirror.[5]

A final symptom is shame. Vanity divides the world into two categories: winners and losers. This means that on the playing field of vanity, when the dust settles, there are only two types of people: the proud and the shamefaced. The majority of people fall into the latter group since few are endowed with all the gifts and opportunities required to meet the ideals of GQ, Forbes, and the Navigators – all at the same time. Thus, if a man desires to avoid the sickbed of self-loathing, he should do everything he can to guard himself against the gangrene of vanity.

Special Tactics for Fighting Vanity

Defensively, the best way to fight vanity is by meditating on the evil, danger, and shame of the passion. The evil of vanity should be obvious after a few minutes of reflection. Think of all of the effort God has made to communicate His love to us and to give us membership into the highest circle in the created order, the divine family. To entertain vanity is to scorn such love. It is the thankless reply, 'I'm sorry, God, but sonship in Christ is inadequate. I need something more if I am to have worth as a human being.' The ugliness of this

---

5. Pascal notes the bizarre way in which human beings prefer the imaginary to the real. He says, 'We do not content ourselves with the life we have in ourselves and in our own being; we desire to live an imaginary life in the mind of others, and for this purpose we endeavor to shine. We labor unceasingly to adorn and preserve this imaginary existence and neglect the real.' See Pascal, *Pensées* (New York: Penguin, 1995), 2.147.

attitude should not take long to calculate. Such ingratitude is and should feel appalling.

Equally, we should think on the shame of vanity. A good exercise is to imagine the final Day of Judgment when each person will give an account of himself to Christ. Here the template of the stewards with the talents is useful. Just imagine that you have to explain to Christ how you invested your time and energy in life. What do you want to say? Do you think Christ will care about the number of 10k races you completed or about the degree certificates framed on your wall? Will you have the self-assurance to hand Christ your resume and say, 'Read this: It speaks for itself!' These are not the things that Christ lived for, and they are not the things He has told us to live for. There is no better way to kill vanity than to recognize the vainness of vanity. The sooner we realize that the coinage of achievement is not legal tender in heaven, the more quickly we will exchange our fool's gold for legitimate treasures.[6]

Finally, men should contemplate the danger of vanity. Shame is not the only outcome of vanity. At times we do succeed in our endeavors and meet the requirements of the world around us. This is not a reason to rejoice, but a reason to watch out. The ego likes nothing more than to feel like it is strong, capable, and better than others. This is how vanity can effortlessly slide into pride. Men should ask whether they want this to happen. Shame or pride, these are the only potential outcomes of vanity. If a man does not like either of these, there is only one thing to do: mortify the passion.[7]

Yet, defense is never sufficient for killing sin. We also need to play aggressive offense. The fact is that there is a kernel of righteousness

---

6. A good verse of Scripture to memorize while wrestling with vanity is Gal. 6:14: 'But far be it from me to boast except in the cross of our Lord Jesus Christ, by which the world has been crucified to me and I to the world.'

7. Thomas Watson warns, 'How many by the wind of popular breath have been blown to Hell.' See *The Body of Divinity*, 'A Preliminary Discourse to Catechising.'

within the crusty exterior of vanity. God has made us with a need to be loved and be found lovely. This need is not sinful. It only becomes sinful when we seek our identity in the wrong community and when we seek our worth in the wrong activity. The key to overcoming vanity, then, is not to try to kill these desires, but rather to seek to fulfill them according to our true design. This means a radical pursuit of meaning and worth through the person and work of Jesus Christ. It is only in Christ that we can hear the voice of the Father say, 'This is my beloved son in whom I am well pleased.'

Equally, it is only through Christ that we find ourselves immersed in a community of love that rejoices in us – not because of the persona we project – but because of the image we reflect.[8] This point needs to be weighed carefully: The more we immerse ourselves in a community that mirrors to us the true virtues and practices of heaven, the less we will find our heart attracted to the empty practices and false virtues of the culture around us.

Target 2: Sloth

Tim is an ordinary, American, twenty-five-year-old guy. When he jumps in the car, he cranks up the radio. When he is standing in a checkout line, he scrolls through his phone. Before going to bed, he

---

8. Men who long for honor and glory should consider the following thought experiment set forth by John Chrysostom, the golden-tongued preacher of the fourth century: 'For what, says He, do you wish? Is it not to have some to be spectators of what is going on? Behold then, you have some; not angels, nor archangels, but the God of all. And if you desire to have men also as spectators, neither of this desire does He deprive you at the fitting season, but rather in greater abundance affords it unto you. For, if you should now make a display, you will be able to make it to ten only, or twenty, or (we will say) a hundred persons: but if you take pains to lie hidden now, God Himself will then proclaim you in the presence of the whole universe. Wherefore above all, if you will have men see your good deeds, hide them now, that then all may look on them with the more honor, God making them manifest, and extolling them, and proclaiming them before all.' See John Chrysostom, *Homilies on Matthew*, available: https://www.newadvent.org/fathers/200119.htm Accessed November 2021.

watches a couple of episodes of something on Netflix. If asked, Tim would not say that he hates silence. However, his choices indicate that solitude is something which he avoids like an uncomfortable itch.

For Tim, work is a necessary evil. A perfect world would be one in which he could seamlessly move from attending a concert to playing a round of golf, from building a deck to having a barbeque with friends. If Tim is addicted to one thing, it is fun. If a genie magically appeared to him and gave him a single wish, it would be that every night could be Saturday night – the lyrics of his favorite country song.

Yet, not all is sunshine and fair weather in Tim's life. Truth be told, he is subject to mood swings that he does not talk about with other people. There are brooding moments when life unexpectedly feels empty and flat. Usually, he tries to skirt these feelings by playing Halo online with friends or going to the gym to work out. Nonetheless, in spite of his efforts, these feelings creep back into his life like a fog. He is not sure what to do about them. His main tactic is to ignore them and wait until they go away.[9]

Tim is a Christian, and he attends church most weekends. Overall, he is a respectable man. He drinks more than he should at some parties and dabbles on websites he knows that he should avoid. However, his lifestyle is more scrupulous than many of his Christian friends. If he could change one thing spiritually, it would be a more consistent daily time with the Lord. The truth is that, if Tim is not at a Christian event, he rarely picks up a Bible or prays in any meaningful way. He knows that his spiritual tank is near empty, but frankly, feels too distracted and busy to fix the problem.

---

[9]. James Davies talks about the potential of our negative feelings to be productive and to draw us into a more honest interaction with life. See James Davies, *The Importance of Suffering: The Value and Meaning of Emotional Discontent* (New York: Routledge, 2012). For a fresh and fascinating look at the causes of depression, see Johann Hari, *Lost Connections: Why You're Depressed and How to Find Hope* (New York: Bloomsbury, 2019).

If we step back from Tim's life, what do we see? Is there a passion that explains the various surface elements of his life? Is he just an average Christian living a normal life, or is there something deeper that needs to be diagnosed? In fact, there is something that is worth bringing to the surface. Tim is in the grip of what an older and wiser generation of Christians would label *acedia*, or to use an English word, *sloth*.[10]

Dissecting Sloth

Sloth is a difficult passion to discuss because there is no English word that captures the essence of the problem. Usually, when we think about slothfulness we tend to think of laziness, a kind of physical or emotional torpor. This condition is thought to be more of the absence of a passion than the presence of one. Yet, this is not the case. Just as boredom is not the lack of feeling, but a weakness of mind, so sloth is not just the absence of passion, but a weakness of the soul.[11] Every adult has been exasperated by a child claiming to be bored while sitting in a room that looks like an aisle of Toys R Us. In such circumstances, the problem is not external to the child, but internal. More than likely the natural curiosity and imagination of the child has been blunted through overstimulation and cheap amusement. Sloth is similar to this. It is a disorder that dampens a man's ability to find joy, satisfaction, and purpose in the greatest good of all, a relationship with the triune God.[12]

---

10. The best recent work on sloth is *The Noonday Devil: Acedia, the Unnamed Evil of Our Times* by Dom Jean-Charles Nault (San Francisco: Ignatius Press, 2015).

11. Dorothy Sayers says, '[Sloth] means the slow sapping of all the faculties by indifference and by the sensation that life is pointless and meaningless and not worthwhile.' See Dorothy Sayers, *The Whimsical Christian* (New York: MacMillan, 1978).

12. Jean-Charles Nault asks, 'But how is it possible that man should be saddened by the prospect of spiritual good, as though that spiritual good were an evil? Acedia is like that, however, and we immediately perceive the gravity of it: acedia is a kind of sadness when faced with spiritual good, which appears to man to be an evil.' See *The Noonday Devil*, p. 71.

In truth, the only way to understand sloth is by thinking about our design. In Genesis we read about Adam and Eve being placed in a garden. They were given a beautiful setting in which to live, work, and enjoy communion with God and one another. Often Christians read the early chapters of Genesis as a description of Paradise. However, I wonder whether the blueprint actually matches the desires of contemporary men. If Christian men were not trying to please their Bible study leaders, they might be asking the following question while reading Genesis 2: *'Wouldn't Adam and Eve get bored?'* (After all, there were no sporting events to attend, no televisions to watch, and no Instagram feeds to scroll.) *How, then, was life in the garden not a primal form of being quarantined?*

The answer to these questions, of course, is that God Himself is inexhaustibly sufficient to satisfy the desires of the human heart. Just as Jesus did not experience loneliness while spending nights in prayer on mountains (much less boredom), Adam and Eve would have had no need for a binge-worthy show because they had something infinitely better – the joy of fellowship with God and the delight of fulfilling the vocation He had given them.

Now the effect of sloth is similar to a grayscale filter on a camera: It removes all color from spiritual goods so that they appear dull, bland, and dissatisfying. Dorothy Sayers says the following about sloth: 'It is the sin that believes in nothing, cares for nothing, enjoys nothing, loves nothing, hates nothing, finds purpose in nothing, lives for nothing, and remains alive only because there is nothing it would die for.'[13] To picture this more concretely, imagine taking a group of teenagers to go and see the Grand Canyon, one of the most majestic landscapes anywhere on the planet. After a long drive, you excitedly tell them to get out of the car. You can't hold back your anticipation. You are the first one to arrive to the edge of the canyon. You pause. Your heart

---

13. See Dorothy Sayers, *Christian Letters to a Post-Christian World: a Selection of Essays* (Grand Rapids: Eerdmans, 1969), p. 152.

soars in wonder and gratitude for the beauty of creation. Grinning like Ronald McDonald, you turn around to see the expressions of the teenagers. The joy dissolves. To your horror, none of the teenagers are even looking. Instead of beholding the grandeur of the landscape, they are playing games and messaging friends on their phones.

This is the effect of sloth, not just on the scale of mere natural beauty, but on the scale of divine glory. In essence, sloth is boredom with God. When sloth fills the heart, the majesty that inspires angels to bow their faces and cry out, 'Holy! Holy! Holy!' is snubbed for nothing better than another round of checking email.

Some may ask whether sloth is that big of a deal. From one angle, it does not seem to result in the heinous crimes that, for example, lust and anger can inspire. However, there is one main reason to fear the sting of sloth. It is this: Sloth is a gateway drug to other hole-filling sins. Augustine's well-rehearsed statement, 'The heart is restless until it rests in you' is not just a cliché of campground talks. It is true. The human heart was made to be filled with the love of God. Jesus makes this clear when He says, 'This is eternal life, that they may know you, the only true God, and Jesus Christ whom you have sent' (John 17:3). When people turn away from God and look to satisfy their deep spiritual needs apart from Him, inevitably lust, greed, and gluttony result. People end up following the pointless itinerary of the prodigal son who looked in the pigsty for what could only be found at his father's table.

The Symptoms of Sloth

Most men will not be accustomed to spotting the symptoms of sloth. One of my children was recently in the hospital due to a burst appendix. The problem was that I didn't recognize the symptoms. What looked to me like a stomach bug was actually something far more dangerous. There is a spiritual truth to pull from this. If we want to kill sin, we need to identify sin. Here are some telltale signs that point to a tumorous growth of sloth.

One is boredom, the feeling that there is nothing meaningful to think about or to do. How men reach this state is hard to understand. Older theologians often talked about God as being the author of two books, one being the book of nature and the other, the Scriptures. Both are stunning revelations of divine glory. In one of Isaac Watts' hymns, he says,

> *Lord, how thy wonders are displayed,*
> *Where're I turn mine eye,*
> *If I survey the ground I tread*
> *Or gaze upon the sky.*
>
> *There's not a plant or flower below*
> *But makes thy glories known,*
> *And clouds arise and tempests blow*
> *By order from thy throne.*

We need to realize that boredom is not just a passing emotion, but a form of illiteracy. One of the two books that God has written will always be within reach. If a man is knowledgeable in how to read both, there will never be a moment when he cannot be communing with God regardless of what else is happening – or isn't happening.[14]

Another is busyness. The great scientist and spiritual writer Pascal said, 'All of humanity's problems stem from man's inability to sit quietly in a room alone.'[15] This statement is justly famous. Pascal was uncovering the uncomfortable truth that a lot of the noise in our lives, as well as the activity in our lives, is a protective measure. We are not just avoiding stillness; we are avoiding God. Sloth likes nothing more than for a soul

---

14. The early Navigators were famous for always having Scripture memory cards in their shirt pockets. Given the fact that modern men always have a phone on their persons, we have no excuse for not filling more of our empty moments with meditation on the Word.

15. Elsewhere Pascal comments that, if men were truly happy (like the angels), they would not be so desperate for amusement. Pascal has a lot more to say on the topic of spiritual boredom. See Pascal, *Pensées*.

to be so agitated that it can never fulfill the gentle instructions, 'Be still and know that I am God.'[16]

Another is emptiness. The heart of a slothful man is a black hole. No matter what goes inside of it, nothing fills it. Modern advertising constantly plays off the insatiable appetite of sloth. Each event, each product, is pitched as must-see or must-have. The promise is always the same: that this is what you need in order to be happy. Yet, the promise never delivers for a single reason: amusement cannot replace worship. The meaning we need cannot be purchased through Amazon. It is a gift that can only come through communion with the Father, Son, and Holy Spirit.[17]

Finally, mediocrity is a symptom of sloth. Worship has a unique ability to amplify the dignity of the soul without producing vanity or pride. The more we know about the majesty of God, the weightier is the calling to be a man. Yet sloth makes us feel as if there is nothing significant to live for. We settle for video games and TV – or for marathons and CrossFit games – because our vision is limited to the horizon of this world. We fail to see that there are some activities in time that can bear the weight of eternity.

It is a sad state of affairs when Saturday night is the highlight of a man's life. Without depreciating the goodness of fun, or the blessing of simple pleasures, men need to know that there are better things to live for. A buttered roll is good, but a sizzling Filet Mignon is better. Watching a hyped football match is fun, but kneeling on a mountaintop in prayer – this is the food of angels.[18]

---

16. The passion of sloth reveals that technology-use is not the cause of distraction, but a symptom of emptiness. The greatest of saints would not be distracted by Instagram, but utterly disinterested in it.

17. Men undervalue the satisfaction of a life of prayer. On prayer, John Chrysostom says: 'One who tastes this food is set on fire with an eternal longing for the LORD: his spirit burns as in a fire of the utmost intensity.' See Chrysostom's wonderful prayer 'Prayer is the Light of the Soul.' Digital copies are available.

18. Thomas Watson says, 'Begin the life of angels here and be in heaven before your time.' See Thomas Watson, *Body of Divinity*, 10.2.

Special Tactics for Killing Sloth

We need to realize that to inhabit the modern world is to attend the school of sloth. Everything around us – from the copy of advertisements to the frenzied notion of a vacation, from the addictive technology in our pockets to our ideals for youth and retirement – all of this is an education in sloth. Nothing in an ordinary week will tell a man to pause his life, to sit quietly on a park bench or in a chapel, and to wait like old Simeon in the temple for the Lord to show up. All of us are addicts. Whether the narcotic of choice is productivity or amusement, the result is the same. We consistently choose the lesser portion by following the frenzy of Martha rather than sitting at the feet of Jesus like Mary.

How do we avoid this? To kill sloth, we need (yet again) to think about playing defense and playing offense. In terms of defense, awareness is no small victory. The more we can decode the world around us, the wiser we will be. As we watch the pre-game show for a playoff game, we need to be aware that something more than a mere introduction is happening. Authoritative voices are telling us that this game cannot be missed – that a historic moment is about to unfold that will never be repeated. Sadly, there is no similar fanfare regarding our quiet times. Somehow skipping a meeting with God feels no more significant than taking a bathroom break during commercials, but to be ignorant of the final score of the Rose Bowl – this is the stuff of unforgivable humiliation.

We need to defend ourselves against such propaganda. There is nothing wrong with fun and amusement. However, as Christians we cannot lose sight that there are greater ends to live for. Our quest in life must always be driven by the passion of Psalm 63:

> O God, you are my God; earnestly I seek you;
> my soul thirsts for you;
> my flesh faints for you,
> as in a dry and weary land where there is no water (v. 1).

In terms of offense, the best way to kill sloth is through a committed pursuit of spiritual disciplines.[19] Honestly, replacing the more vacuous activities of life with things like Bible reading, prayer, worship, service, and meditation (on the Word) will not feel like replacing water with Red Bull, but Red Bull with water. Rather than having a sudden rush of spiritual energy, the disciplines themselves may at first feel tedious and life-sapping. Some men may find themselves experiencing the five stages of grief as they cut the cable and pick up the Bible. This is to be expected. The road to recovery is never easy. Yet, some destinations are worth the difficulty of the journey getting there. This is uniquely true of knowing God. Here David provides expert testimony. As a warrior and as a king, David experienced everything the world has to offer: adventure, success, heroism, love, vast building projects, public esteem – the list hardly ends. Yet, what was the one thing that he said was better than life? Not sex. Not fun. Not building a legacy. His answer was the love of God (cf. Ps. 63:3). This is the lesson that the spiritual disciplines will teach us.[20]

---

19. This is where an older generation of Christians would give some stern advice. In *The Christian Soldier*, Thomas Watson encourages a kind of holy violence toward oneself. He says, 'Provoking ourselves to duty, implies a uniting, and rallying together of all the powers of our soul, setting them on work in the exercises of religion. A man says to his thoughts, be you fixed on God in this duty; and to his affections, do you serve the Lord without distraction? Matters of religion must be done with intenseness of spirit.' Similarly, Bernard of Clairvaux says, 'Therefore when you feel weighed down by apathy, lukewarmness and fatigue, do not yield to cowardice or cease to study spiritual truths, but look for the hand of the one who can help you, begging like the bride, to be drawn, until finally, under the influence of grace, you feel again the vigorous pulse of life.' See Bernard of Clairvaux, *Sermons on Song of Songs* (Kindle edition).

20. Discipline and desire should go hand in hand. Augustine says, 'The entire life of a good Christian is in fact an exercise of holy desire. You do not yet see what you long for, but the very act of desiring prepares you, so that when he comes you may see and be utterly satisfied.' Augustine, *On the First Letter of John*.

Target 3: Lust

Lust does not require as much of an introduction as vanity and sloth. No effort is needed to persuade men that lust is a toxin present in their bloodstream. We can, therefore, limit our discussion to two critical questions: First, what exactly is lust? Second, how do we kill it?

As is true of other sins, to understand lust we need to understand our design. Human beings are *persons* made in the image of God. This means that we were made to show and receive love and respect. Human beings have a remarkable ability to enjoy communion, which is a spiritual mingling of souls. Yet, such communion can only happen when we honor the dignity of other people and freely choose to love them, not use them. To reduce another person to a mere object is to eliminate the possibility of love. From that point on, he or she is treated as a tool for selfish gain rather than a child of God to be served.

Human sexuality finds its meaning and purpose within this basic design. Sexuality was never intended by God to be a means of individual fulfillment; it is a special gift through which human beings fulfill their calling to love in a context of commitment and fidelity. Sexual desire and marriage thus go hand in hand. Marriage is the unique means through which a man and woman discover an intimacy, giving of self, and total communication that mysteriously reflects the triune life of God.[21]

We need this background to see the evil of lust. Lust is the attitude that reduces another person to his or her sexual value. With lust, love and respect are dumped in the rubbish bin. I do not care about the happiness of another person. I do not seek to promote their good or to preserve their dignity. Instead, I long to consume them like I

---

21. Roman Catholic theologians, especially Pope John Paul II, have done a particularly good job exploring the nature of human sexuality. A simple book that gleans much of this insight is *The Theology of the Body in One Hour* by Jason Evert (Scottsdale: Totus Press, 2017).

would consume a bucket of chicken from KFC. They are an object for conquest; not a sister – or brother – to cherish.

There are several startling implications once we understand what lust is. One is the scary truth that lust can occur even within the context of marriage. It is not uncommon for a husband to care more about gratifying his own sexual appetite than loving and serving his wife. In such moments, the motive for sex is not self-giving love, the basis of all godliness, but self-serving lust, the basis of all idolatry. We need to be aware that while sex is a holy gift within marriage, not all sex within marriage is holy.

Another implication is that the goal of purity is not simply avoiding lust, but learning how to love. A lot of men fight sexual temptation merely by trying to avert their eyes. They do their best to resist the urge to look at pornography, to objectify women in the workplace, or to indulge in private fantasies. Yet, avoiding contamination will never result in the purity of heart that is required to kill lust. In order to be pure, men must change not only what they look at, but how they see. They must not only avoid looking at women, but learn how to look at women. Yes, this means that men must flee from pornography as they would flee from a cloud of nerve gas. But it also means something far more challenging: men must look upon all women as they would look upon their mothers and upon their sisters – as persons of hallowed worth and dignity.

So, then, how does a man kill lust? The answer is a combination of Romans 13:14 and Matthew 6:22.[22] On the one hand, he can make no provision for his flesh (cf. Rom. 13:14). He must toe the line of fanaticism in his efforts to cut out known sources of temptation. Men can hardly be too relentless in this effort. Although there is nothing new under the sun, there has never been a culture more saturated

---

22. For more detailed advice on combatting lust and growing in purity see Ted Roberts, *Pure Desire: Helping People Break Free from Sexual Struggles* (Ventura: Regal, 1999). Another useful ministry to investigate is Broken Strength: https://www.apathtopurity.org/ Accessed November 2021.

in myths and rituals regarding sex than our own culture is.[23] All of the messaging around us repeats the lie that our deepest fulfillment depends upon indulging our sexual desires. We are even told that our identity depends more than anything else on sexual preferences. And – as if things could not get any worse – the internet has made all forms of pornography both ubiquitous and free. If a man does not vehemently and constantly resist the gravity of this culture, he will succumb to it. Resistance will be no small part of our victory over lust.[24]

Yet, as mentioned above, looking away cannot replace looking anew. Jesus says, 'The eye is the lamp of the body. So, if your eye is healthy, your whole body will be full of light' (Matt. 6:22). The question is, how do we clean the eyes of the heart so that, instead of living in the chains of darkness, we can walk in the freedom of the light?

There are two primary ways to refine our vision. One way is through beholding the beauty of holiness. Elsewhere, Jesus says, 'Blessed are the pure in heart, for they shall see God' (Matt. 5:8). This statement can be read front to back or back to front. On the one hand, it says that purity of heart is the condition that enables the vision of God. On the other, that the vision of God is what purifies the heart. Both readings are correct. The key application for us is this: the more we pause to meditate on the holiness of God, the purer our hearts will be. Such purity will then translate into a freedom to praise God for the beauty of women (which after all He did create) without itching to consume women like lions watching a herd of gazelles.

---

23. For a magisterial treatment of the role of sex in modern society see Carl Trueman, *The Rise and Triumph of the Modern Self: Cultural Amnesia, Expressive Individualism, and the Road to Sexual Revolution* (Wheaton: Crossway, 2020). For a more accessible entry point to the topic, see Glynn Harrison, *A Better Story: God, Sex, and Human Flourishing* (London: IVP, 2016).

24. Thomas Chalmers says, 'The humility which leads us to flee whenever we can, and to pray when flight is impossible – this is the very habit of the soul, which removes it from the first set of temptations, and will most effectually strengthen it against the second.' See *Lectures on Romans, Vol.2*, p. 149.

But second, we can also retrain our minds to think differently about women. As suggested above, there is one relationship that men have with women that almost never gets reduced to sexual terms. This is the relationship that a man has with his sisters. Why is this? The reason is not because sisters are not beautiful. The reason, rather, is because there is a no trespassing fence in the mind that says, 'Here is a woman whose dignity must be respected and preserved at all costs.' There is no reason why we should limit this fence line to our near relations. Instead, we ought to learn to view all women as sisters first and accordingly show them the respect and love that we owe them as their brothers.[25]

Target 4: Pride

An entire set of encyclopedias could be written about pride. This is the big daddy of sins, the one that sires, feeds, and nurtures the other ones. I do not want to attempt here an exhaustive profile of pride. Information overload is a poor method of training. Instead, I want to highlight a particular pattern of pride that is a clear and present danger to contemporary men.

The essence of pride is setting me before God. The proud man looks to Jesus, who receives endless praise from all of the angels, and clenches his teeth. He longs to wave a hand in the air and say, 'Hey angels, could a couple of you turn my way for a minute or two? Could you sing a few, loud choruses of "Hail Joe!" for everyone else to hear?'

---

25. Jason Evert offers a very helpful practice that men can adopt to defend against lust. He recommends that when a man is tempted by the beauty of a woman to lust after her he should inconspicuously make the sign of the cross and go through four mental actions: (1) he should look up (mentally) and give thanks to God for the gift of beauty; (2) he should look down and confess the lust that is in his heart; (3) he should glance to the side, remember the dignity of the woman, and pray a blessing upon her; and (4) he should glance to the other side and celebrate the truth that our deepest desires will be fulfilled in God Himself. For more on this see Jason Evert, *The Dating Blueprint* (Scotsville: Totus Press, 2019), p. 22ff.

As ugly as it sounds, a lust for preeminence is the heartbeat of pride. If there was a way of shoving God off of the throne of glory, this is exactly what pride would do.

Now there is a hard form and a soft form of such self-centeredness. The hard form is shown in the attitude of Pharaoh in the Old Testament. No one has said 'No!' to God more trenchantly than Pharaoh did. Even after ten plagues – and a dead son – he would not tap out. It took the weight of the entire Red Sea to bury his ego.

Yet, pride does not always result in such steely rebellion. A softer form is seen in the heart of another Old Testament character, Balaam. Balaam did not question the sovereignty of the Living God. God was God; Balaam was not. But Balaam did coddle the hope that he could manipulate God. He thought that, like a dog on a leash, he could tell God where to go.

Now I don't want to consider here the pride of Pharaoh. Once a man reaches such a hardened condition there is little that can be done for him. Instead, I want to examine the pride of Balaam, because this softer form of me-centeredness is a standard ingredient in the psychology of modern men. As briefly as possible, I want to run through the typical education of pride in the twenty-first century. This summary will be like the tilted mirror used by dentists. It will reveal back crevices of the heart that otherwise are nearly impossible to see.

The Curriculum of Pride

The schooling of pride begins at the dawn of consciousness when a child is bathed in a sea of platitudes that tell him that the center of the solar system is not the sun, or God, but the self. Every Disney movie, every board-covered book, repeats a similar message: be true to yourself, follow your heart, the key to fulfillment is within you. Behind these ideas is a glorious conceit: that the world is a stage, that life is a play, and that I have been chosen to be the lead actor. The child learns early that parents, grandparents, and teachers are not founts of wisdom, but instruments of applause. The job of everyone with wrinkles on their eyes is to set the stage so that I can act out my self-appointed destiny.

The next stage of development comes through technology and social media. Social media takes an assumed belief – the conviction that I am the center of the world – and makes it a reality. Already in pre-adolescence I am given something that in former days only kings, priests, and prophets had access to, a platform. Suddenly, I can speak authoritatively about any issue on my mind and watch as friends and even strangers react to my trumpeting.[26]

Meanwhile, a further stage of growth is happening. There was a time when marketing was focused on demonstrating the quality of a product. That stone-age is gone. The agenda of marketeers today is to cast the customer as the hero of his own story. Gatorade is no longer a salt-laden drink to satisfy thirst. It is the nectar of gods that enables men to perform Herculean feats. Thus, advertising feeds into the same river as technology and talk-show therapy. They all combine to fill a vast reservoir of self-importance.

This education continues as teenagers 'adult.' As video games are put aside for podcasts and audiobooks, fresh winds of pop psychology begin to blow. Life management gurus preach a thousand variations of the same message: that the goal of life – and the key to happiness – is to write your own script. For this to happen, there is one golden rule: I must put myself before others. If I do not love myself, others cannot be loved. If my happiness account is in the red, there will be no surplus to share with others. All of this leads to one 'irrefutable' conclusion: my number one priority in life must be *me*. Service is good, but emotional health is better. To lose sight of this is to drift into unhappiness.[27]

---

26. See David Brooks section on 'The Big Me' in *The Road to Character* (New York: Random House, 2016).

27. C. J. Mahaney describes our cultural recipe for greatness as follows: 'Individuals motivated by self-interest, self-indulgence and a false sense of self-

So, where does this leave us? What is the cumulative effect of this education on a man by the time he reaches middle age? In short, he has swallowed the hook of Balaam. With absolute sincerity he believes two dangerous lies. One is that he is the center of the universe. The other is that, if there is a god – a belief he is not quite sure of – then the chief responsibility of this god must be to be *my* personal genie. After all, every Luke Skywalker needs a Yoda, and the picture that a lot of Christian men have of 'god' is not far off from a small, cuddly alien who specializes in launching the careers of future Jedis.

The Symptoms of Pride

The point of the summary above is not to point the finger at a few men, but to cast a net over all of us. Like fluoride in the waterlines, this education is unavoidable. All of us are contaminated by the psychology of self-centeredness. This means that it is of utmost importance that we recognize when these lies reach critical levels in our thinking. Here are symptoms to watch out for.

First, anger. Pride and a deep-seated sense of entitlement always go hand in hand. The person who views God as a genie genuinely believes that *my* wish is God's command. Thus, if wishes go unfulfilled, resentment brews. I feel as if I have a right to be angry with God because He has not ratified my desires for health, wealth, and prosperity.

Second is self-worship. Since the advent of social media, we have collectively forgotten that the goal of maturity is not self-promotion, but self-effacement. The Son does not glorify Himself; He brings glory to the Father. The Spirit does not glorify Himself; He brings glory to the Son. How, then, do we feel at peace to build a digital platform and mount a golden statue of 'me' at the crest of it? This is not the child of humility, but of pride. Only pride would make us

---

sufficiency pursue selfish ambitions for the purpose of self-glorification.' See Mahaney, *Humility: True Greatness*, p. 44.

care more about attracting our own followers rather than making followers of Christ.

Third is greed. Greed is prioritizing things before both God and other people. There is nothing wrong with desiring to achieve excellence in the workplace. However, if this desire leads me to sacrifice the stillness of my soul before God, or my responsibility to disciple my children, then greed has set in. I now care more about the things of success than the things of the Spirit. At the root of such greed is always a me-focused attitude. I cannot prioritize things before God, or things before people, unless I first prioritize myself above all.[28]

How to Kill Pride

There would be nothing more futile than trying to provide a simple method for killing pride. If pride is the deepest sin, it is also the hardest to kill. Therefore, the best advice I can offer is to re-read the chapter on killing deadly passions and to think specifically about how to apply those instructions to the roots of pride.[29]

What I can offer here are some suggestions about specific lines of meditation that will be helpful for shifting the gaze of the heart away from the self and toward God.

First, men who hate their pride should invest long tracts of time meditating on the majesty of God. My advice would be to camp out in Isaiah 40 until the holiness of God sweeps you off of your feet and grinds your nose into the ground. The self is a mesmerizing object to look at. We all know from Zoom calls that it is nearly impossible to have

---

28. Envy is a related symptom. The vain ego laments to see the success and prosperity of other people. Vanity is saddened when peers advance further than I do. The reason for this is that vanity always follows the logic of a zero-sum game. For others to increase, I must decrease, and the vain self cannot be humbled and happy at the same time.

29. This is why the case study of Steve focused on pride. This passion needs to be targeted above and beyond any other.

our own reflections on a screen without ending up staring at ourselves. The only way to break this spell is to turn off all screens and to shift our attention to something infinitely more fascinating. Isaiah 40 is a glass in which we can marvel at the immensity of God.[30] As He expands to immeasurable dimensions, something else will be happening in the heart: our ego will quietly deflate. Rather than believing the balloonish dimensions of our imagination, we will be cut back to our actual size. Humility will begin to set in.

Second, men need to flip the script of modern life-coaching. Rather than casting ourselves as the hero of our stories, we need to adopt an altogether different posture, that of a slave. We need to realize that for Christ to increase, we must decrease; for Christ to be lord, we must be servants. This is not just a mental exercise. It is an attitude that must be lived daily. There is no surer way to cut down pride than to live out each day in a spirit of total availability. The man who starts each day – not with the assertion, 'My will be done!' but with the prayer, 'Speak, Lord, Your servant is listening,' – is on the long road that leads to humility.[31]

Finally, to kill pride we need to reflect deeply on the grace of God. Nothing kills an attitude of entitlement more readily than realizing that the only things that we deserve are condemnation and eternal punishment.[32] This is a truth that grace prompts us to remember. Yet, grace does more than this. It replaces the spirit of entitlement with an

---

30. Walt Henrichsen explores in further detail how Isaiah 40 can change our perspective of both man and God. See chapter 4 in *Disciples Are Made, Not Born* (Colorado Springs: David C. Cook, 2011).

31. Embodied practices are needed to kill pride. Nothing de-centers the self more quickly than going out and serving other people. There is a spiritual joy that comes from service, one which unsettles the superficial contentment of pride. Through concrete acts of love, we begin to experience the truth that our good comes from serving others, not from serving ourselves (cf. Mark 10:45).

32. Carl Henry was once asked how he had stayed humble in the midst of so many accomplishments. His reply was this: 'How can anyone be arrogant when he stands beside the cross?'

unpayable debt of gratitude. My recommendation to men who need help recovering their sense of indebtedness to God is to set apart an hour to reflect on the following hymn by Robert Murray M'Cheyne.

> *When this passing world is done,*
> *When has sunk yon glaring sun,*
> *When we stand with Christ on high*
> *Looking o'er life's history,*
> *Then, Lord, shall I fully know,*
> *Not till then, how much I owe.*
>
> *When I hear the wicked call*
> *On the rocks and hills to fall,*
> *When I see them start and shrink*
> *On the fiery deluge brink,*
> *Then, Lord, shall I fully know,*
> *Not till then, how much I owe.*
>
> *When I stand before the throne,*
> *Dressed in beauty not my own,*
> *When I see thee as thou art,*
> *Love thee with unsinning heart,*
> *Then, Lord, shall I fully know,*
> *Not till then, how much I owe.*
>
> *When the praise of heav'n I hear,*
> *Loud as thunders to the ear,*
> *Loud as many waters' noise,*
> *Sweet as harp's melodious voice,*
> *Then, Lord, shall I fully know,*
> *Not till then, how much I owe.*
>
> *Chosen not for good in me,*
> *Wakened up from wrath to flee,*
> *Hidden in the Savior's side,*
> *By the Spirit sanctified,*
> *Teach me, Lord, on earth to show,*
> *By my love, how much I owe.*

Epilogue

◁◁♦♦▷▷

On the eve of what looked to be the darkest hour in the history of the United Kingdom, Winston Churchill aired his unforgettable Dunkirk speech on the radio. The most famous lines from the speech are the following:

> Even though large tracts of Europe and many old and famous States have fallen or may fall into the grip of the Gestapo and all the odious apparatus of Nazi rule, we shall not flag or fail. We shall go on to the end, we shall fight in France, we shall fight on the seas and oceans, we shall fight with growing confidence and growing strength in the air, we shall defend our Island, whatever the cost may be, we shall fight on the beaches, we shall fight on the landing grounds, we shall fight in the fields and in the streets, we shall fight in the hills; we shall never surrender.

It's nearly impossible to read these lines without a surge of adrenalin stirring the heart. It would be tempting to end a book on fighting sin using these words as a call to resist the aggression of sin wherever it may be encountered. Yet, for Christians, the most interesting lines from Churchill's speech are actually those which immediately follow the above quotation:

> …and even if, which I do not for a moment believe, this Island or a large part of it were subjugated and starving, then our Empire beyond

the seas, armed and guarded by the British Fleet, would carry on the struggle, until, in God's good time, the New World, with all its power and might, steps forth to the rescue and the liberation of the old.

It is these lines that capture with stunning accuracy the vision that sustains Christians in the midst of what often feels like a losing battle against sin. Ultimately, our hope is not in advancing the trench line of godliness a few inches here, a few there. If this were all that we had to look forward to, combat fatigue would quickly incapacitate the soul and leave us paralyzed on the battlefield. No, our eyes must always be on a greater victory, something that will only occur when 'the New World, with all its power and might, steps forth to the rescue and the liberation of the old.' This was the hope of Paul, the confidence that drove him to endure all, surrender all, and suffer all for the sake of Christ, and this needs to be our hope. We carry on the fight, not because we think our efforts will amount to any stunning victory. The hope is otherwise. We look forward to the day when God will do for us what we could never do for ourselves, when the final victory is so complete that sin and death are not just defeated, but gone forever.

So, then, where does this leave us? What is the last word that should be given to a pilgrim who has just been handed a sword and who is about to continue on a long and dangerous journey?

Millennia ago there was a battle between various Greek city-states. On the one side stood the Spartans and their allies; on the other, the Argives and theirs. Each of the commanders for the various armies took a turn before the battle giving a speech to his soldiers. On the side of the Argives, a Mantanaen general stood up and urged his men to remember their country and to fight valiantly lest they all return to slavery. In a word, this general appealed to the emotions of loyalty and fear in order to stir his troops to action. He hoped these feelings would sustain them in battle.

EPILOGUE

Next it was the turn of the Argive's leader. His rallying cry was this: To punish the Spartans for the thousands of wrongs that they had committed. Here was an appeal to hatred and anger in order to motivate forceful aggression. Again, the strategy was to fuel action using emotion.

The other side of the field was a lot quieter. Yes, the Spartan general also stood up to speak, but in typical Spartan fashion his words were few. He simply said, 'Men, *remember your training*.'[1]

The Spartans knew something that a lot of Christian men would benefit from learning. Emotion is a poor man's substitute for motivation. In the heat of battle, training goes a lot farther than a fiery pep talk. All of us need to keep this in mind as we step into the arena against sin. We cannot depend upon any particular feeling to carry us forward. It will be training, not emotion, that keeps us in the fight. Prayer, vigilance, meditation, and repentance – these are the core tactics of killing sin. They are the practices that empty the heart of self-reliance and keep the knees bent before the Throne of Grace. Remember them and your efforts will not be in vain.

> *Therefore we do not lose heart. Even though our outward man is perishing, yet the inward man is being renewed day by day. For our light affliction, which is but for a moment, is working for us a far more exceeding and eternal weight of glory, while we do not look at the things which are seen, but at the things which are not seen. For the things which are seen are temporary, but the things which are not seen are eternal.*
>
> (2 Cor. 4:16-18, NKJV)

---

1. For the details of the story see Thucydides, *The Peloponnesian War*, 5.66-74.

Appendix:
Simple Next Steps

◁◁♦♦▷▷

There is nothing worse than finishing a book, having learned a lot of information, but having no clear next steps to translate theory into practice. Here are seven actions related to the book that ordinary men can start implementing right now.

1. *Start Your Day by Praying through St. Patrick's Breastplate*

    Mindset is critical for fighting sin. By praying St. Patrick's Breastplate, or even just a segment of the prayer, a man will begin his day in a spirit of vigilance. This prayer can be found at the end of chapter two of this book.

2. *Buy a Notebook and Journal Key Insights regarding Temptation and Sinful Passions*

    Self-knowledge is hard won. Remember the case study of Steve. Insight into entrenched sin requires sustained reflection. Don't be content with a vague sense that you struggle with lust or pride. Ask probing questions: When do I struggle? What triggers spark my struggle? What lies am I believing that reinforce my struggle? What desires are beneath my struggle? Intelligence regarding sin must be gathered in order to fight sin intelligently.

3. *Take Responsibility for Your Environment*

    Changing our environment will never kill sin. However, it can reduce temptation. Are you setting yourself up for failure? If so, use common sense. Remove obvious triggers that lead to temptation.

4. *Find a Friend Who Can See Your Shadow*

We all have a shadow, but most of the time we cannot see it. This is the problem with relying on self-examination to deal with sin. I will be oblivious to what is obvious to a friend. Find someone who can hold you accountable, support you in temptation, and encourage you toward virtue. To fight alone is to set yourself up for failure.

5. *Memorize the Ten Rules of War*

We all hate memorizing stuff, but the following point is undeniable: What we remember, we retain. Do you want to fight sin? If so, memorize the key principles that will enable you to fight with courage and resolve.

6. *Diagnose Your Mindset*

In chapter three, a lot of lies were discussed. Which ones are currently influencing you? Re-read the headings in the chapter and use the information to test the state of your mind regarding sin and temptation.

7. *Sign Up for CT 12*

A lot of men struggle to grow spiritually because they don't have a plan for growth. CT 12 is a twelve-week program by Cross Training Ministries that focuses on simple routines, bodily discipleship, and spiritual friendship. Men who do this program will not only be helped in developing good habits that promote spiritual growth; they will also be helped in breaking bad habits that impede spiritual growth. You can find out more about this program at www.menneedhelp.org.

The Way Forward

A Road Map of Spiritual Growth for Men in the 21st Century

Joe Barnard

A lot of Christian men – and small groups of men – feel stuck. They have a sincere desire to grow but feel confused about what to do next. The Way Forward is a road-map for men who want to cut through the noise and distraction of the twenty-first century and take definite steps toward spiritual maturity. This book follows the simple format of problem, solution, and plan. Men who read it will walk away with both a clear diagnosis for why they feel stuck and a practical action plan for moving forward.

Jesus calls His followers to be disciples who make disciples. Men and women face similar and distinct challenges in obeying Christ's command. The Way Forward provides a fresh look at the obstacles and opportunities men face as they seek to be built up into the image of Christ.

J. Garrett Kell
Pastor, Del Ray Baptist Church, Alexandria, Virginia

978-1-5271-0467-9

Christian Focus Publications

Our mission statement —

STAYING FAITHFUL

In dependence upon God we seek to impact the world through literature faithful to His infallible Word, the Bible. Our aim is to ensure that the Lord Jesus Christ is presented as the only hope to obtain forgiveness of sin, live a useful life and look forward to heaven with Him.

Our books are published in four imprints:

CHRISTIAN FOCUS
Popular works including biographies, commentaries, basic doctrine and Christian living.

CHRISTIAN HERITAGE
Books representing some of the best material from the rich heritage of the church.

MENTOR
Books written at a level suitable for Bible College and seminary students, pastors, and other serious readers. The imprint includes commentaries, doctrinal studies, examination of current issues and church history.

CF4•K
Children's books for quality Bible teaching and for all age groups: Sunday school curriculum, puzzle and activity books; personal and family devotional titles, biographies and inspirational stories — because you are never too young to know Jesus!

Christian Focus Publications Ltd,
Geanies House, Fearn, Ross-shire,
IV20 1TW, Scotland, United Kingdom.
www.christianfocus.com